8

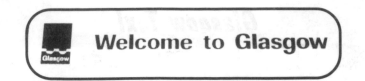

Welcome to Glasgow

This is the bird that never flew,

This is the tree that never grew,

This is the bell that never rang,

This is the fish that never swam.

Let Glasgow Taxis Flourish

Glasgow Taxi

JACK CLYDE

SHEPHEARD-WALWYN (PUBLISHERS) LTD

© Jack Clyde 2004

First published in 2004 by
Shepheard-Walwyn (Publishers) Ltd
Suite 604, The Chandlery
50 Westminster Bridge Road
London SE1 7QY

British Library Cataloguing in Publication Data
A catalogue record of this book
is available from the British Library

ISBN 0 85683 232 4

Typeset by Alacrity
Banwell Castle, Weston-super-Mare
Printed through Creative Print & Design (Wales) Ltd, Ebbw Vale

Contents

———————————3———————————

THE GLASGOW TAXI TRADE

Acknowledgements

My sincere thanks to the following for helping me along the way:

The Mitchell Library, Glasgow, in particular the staff in the Glasgow Room
Ms Alex Robertson, Curator of the Glasgow Transport Museum
Barr's Irn-Bru
The Glasgow Transport Museum
Glasgow Taxis Committee
CLN Taxi Repairs (Shawfield)
Clyde Taxi Advertising (Glasgow)
Sam's Carwash (Shawfield)
John Cassidy (taxi enthusiast)
Loop Graphic Design & Print (Glasgow)
Anna Blair (author)
David O'Hare
The London Cab Trade by Phillip Warren
A History of the London Taxicab by G.N. Georgano
Taxi by Simon Garner & Giles Stokoe
History of King's Park and Surrounding Areas
Old Shettleston by J.F. Miller
Scottish Memories
The Western Leader
The Daily Record
On Rank magazine
The Flag magazine

$$\sim 1 \sim$$

Introducing Myself

I, John Swan Clyde, was born on December 12 1951 in the bedroom of my grandmother's ground floor flat at 445 St Vincent Street, Anderston in Glasgow.

Or, as Billy Connolly would say, 'That quaint little fishing village on the Clyde.'

My father and mother stayed at the same address, only three stairs up.

The 'old' Glasgow Savings Bank in Argyle Street, Anderston. 445 St Vincent Street lay directly behind it, where the concrete flats can now be seen.

My mother Cathie and my father Archie both worked, my mother for the Co-op, serving behind the counter throughout the years of the Second World War. She was refused permission to join the WRAF as she was deemed to be doing a man's job. She left working life to have a family, me in 1951, my sister Gloria in 1954, then returned to work – this time for the Glasgow Corporation as a home help – and stayed thirty years, until retiring at the age of 60.

My father worked full-time after leaving school at the age of 14. He started with the City Bakeries but joined the RAF at the start of the war and spent his years of conscription as a driver – driving everything from motorbikes to the 'Queen Mary' (the equivalent of today's low loader transport for recovering fighter aircraft unable to make it safely home).

After the war he returned to the bakery and stayed until the age of 27. Then he left and bought his first Glasgow taxi. This was in 1949. By the time I arrived in 1951 he had built his business up from one cab to three.

We stayed at St Vincent Street until I was 8, then moved to Jordanhill in Glasgow's West End, to a three-bedroom semi facing a playing field. 'A home of your own built by John Lawrence.'

It was here I had most fun. I played football in the field opposite and explored the woods with new friends and neighbours. It was great.

My father having increased the size of his small fleet of cabs to eight, and his brother Peter having come into the trade, followed by Uncle Bernard, I was always in the company of taxi drivers. From the age of 8 I helped my father and mother clean the taxis before they went for their annual 'inspection'. It was a job they both took very seriously and carried out together with great pride. Neighbours and passers-by would comment on the immaculate condition of our cabs. To this day the same standards apply, and we still earn the praise of the public.

In 1960 my job was to clean 'the steels' with a Brillo pad. These were the chrome or alloy strips that ran along the running boards of the old FX3. After that I was directed to an hour of scrubbing out the open luggage compartment which had picked up all the dirt and scrapes imaginable.

The old tenements on St Vincent Street where I spent my earliest

My father Archie and me outside 445 St Vincent Street in 1954

years were just over a mile from the Central Station. Anderston was a working-class area, the majority of its men toiling in the ship-yards or docks down the road on Clydeside. The buses and trams passed right by our building. St Vincent Street was a hub of activity.

Everyone knew everyone else in the neighbourhood. There wasn't much money about but there was a good feeling, a cama-raderie in the community. In true Glasgow spirit, if people fell on hard times there'd be a whip-round to pull them out of a hole.

The docks were busy and there was always a bargain to be had from your local docker in the form of 'excess cargo' – goods that supposedly couldn't fit into the ship! (No, even then I found that one a little hard to swallow.)

Did you know that the weight of an export bottle of whisky is exactly the same as a common house brick?

*

3

Kelvingrove Park was less than half a mile from our close. It had a fascinating art gallery which I visited almost every week and there was a big stone fountain with faces staring out at you as water cascaded from their mouths into a pool where you could sail your toy yacht or motor boat. If you were thirsty there was the Lion drinking fountain with a cup on a chain.

The fountain in Kelvingrove Park.

The park had wonderful play areas. In the swing park there was a huge chute as well as swings and roundabouts and the all-important maypole where I had so much difficulty hanging on.

Hill 60 was the biggest hill in the park, great fun for playing 'Best man dives' or just rolling down. It was the best hill in the world at Easter time when we all made our way there to 'roll an egg'.

The park was always splendidly presented – pride was taken by the gardeners who tended to the seasonal needs of its 85 acres. At the far side was the charming Art Gallery, the most beautiful building I've seen in all my life. As a small boy I ignored the paintings, I was fascinated by all the stuffed animals and the armoury gallery with knights in shining armour with two-handled swords (that looked like you'd need to call Pickfords to swing at anything).

The Kelvingrove Art Gallery and Museum, opened in 1901

The working beehive and the dinosaur exhibition also kept me amused for ages, but the jewel in the crown was most definitely the model ships. A whole room was devoted to these works of art, many of which had been made as their mother ships were being built in the Glasgow shipyards. They've now been moved to the Clyde Room at the Transport Museum opposite the Art Gallery and people from all over the world come to admire the superb scale models ... it's a priceless exhibition.

HMS Hood, the flagship of the British Royal Navy sunk in 1942 in Scapa Flow with the loss of nearly two thousand men

I had started school at Partickhill Primary when I was 5. That was a private school with a tight curriculum where I was constantly under pressure. Our move to Jordanhill meant a change of school – to Bankhead Primary in Knightswood. This brought out the worst in me. I was easily influenced and having fallen in with the wrong crowd, the standard of my work dropped dramatically in my first year. I became unruly and lost all respect for schooling. Things improved when I moved to Broomhill School when I was 10. It took a while, but a better teacher, Mrs Brown, and a more civilised class brought me back into line.

Outside school, I helped with the garden and was keen to be involved in my father's business. He gave me the job of counting the money from the drivers' 'weigh-ins'. I'd open the envelopes containing the cash that had been taken and check it was correct. Then all the banknotes were put into piles so that I could sort them into bundles of twenty for the bank teller – they were spread out on the floor as if a big jig-saw puzzle was under construction. The piles of Scottish notes were always much larger than the piles of English notes.

Sometimes a driver's money included American dollars and we'd know he'd taken American sailors to Greenock or Gourock, probably returning them to their ship after a night on the town. In those days the exchange rate was three dollars to the pound.

I always enjoyed the drivers' calling at the house, their patter and their stories about that hire they'd had last week.

At 13 I captured a coveted job as a milk boy with Stotts' Dairies in Whittingham Drive, Anniesland. This was to be my introduction to big money – £2/10/- a week! My shift started at 3am when milk was loaded onto the cart and the driver would hitch up the horse. About 4am we'd set off in the open cart, destination Partick.

That winter it was unbelievably cold. Despite the excellent money on offer I managed to stick the job for only four days.

By this time my father was running a taxi garage, repairing and servicing taxis. I started selling diesel at the pumps on Saturday afternoons, and in school holidays was upgraded to general 'go-fur' and 'T boy'. I loved working with the men in the garage and never tired of the 'crack' between mechanics and panel-beaters. The football and religious rivalries between the two departments were comical. Only in Glasgow is the mixture of religion and football so lethal.

Proudly placed above the mechanics' pits for all to see was a picture of William of Orange on his white horse in 1690. On each side of this shrine were laid two orange lilies, and there was a bonnet with an orange-and-white plume (just worn by an apprentice mechanic in the 'Orange Walk', the parade celebrating the split from the Roman Catholic Church).

The body shop, not to be outdone, worked beneath an overhanging banner of the Pope blessing the crowd in the Vatican City. A small tin fixed to the wall below the banner symbolised the fount of holy water. A Celtic scarf was draped over the top. This scarf is the common denominator – it unites the football and the religion.

Friday was pay-day and on Friday night mechanics and body-shop workers would go for a drink together in one of the local bars. Friday night was always good. Saturday was another matter. Saturday was football day. Club rivalry reasserted itself and the Friday night camaraderie was flushed away.

*

Sadly the garage closed when I was 18 and I had to look elsewhere for work. I was still too young to enter the Glasgow cab trade where there was a minimum age limit of 21. My father's drivers told me about a new taxi company in the East End of Glasgow (just yards outside the city limits), the Blue Star Line, owned by two colourful ex-Glasgow taxi drivers called McGregor and McCully.

I started work with them almost immediately, driving my father's 1966 Ford Zodiac MkIII, JGA 53D. It was a beautiful Saluki Bronze metallic colour with black interior – very impressive. Thinking back, this wonderful car was sold to me very cheaply, no doubt as compensation for the closing of the garage. It guarangeed me an instant job start.

Driving for Blue Star Line in Shettleston I gained considerable knowledge of the East End of the city. BSL had no two-way radio system; each driver had to return to the office and wait his turn for the next job.

My Zodiac doubled as a wedding car. Times were changing. People wanted something more up-to-date than the traditional Hackney Carriage which had done the job since the early days of the FX3. I'd transform the Zodiac for a wedding by removing 'Taxi' from the roof, putting a flower display in the rear window and fresh ribbons on the front and draping a crisp white sheet over the back seat. I would receive the princely fee of £5, a good price for the punter and a good rate for me – in fact a full day's wages for just a couple of hours' work.

After working the East End for 6 months I went to Z Cars in East Kilbride. There I was absolutely shafted. Still very green, I signed a contract with the owner of the radio company but it transpired that all the facts and figures I'd been given were lies or, at best, distortions. I'll avoid telling a tale a mile long and just say I personally was lumbered with a loan for thousands. It left me feeling extremely bitter – likewise the other owner-drivers who'd had a similar experience.

Travelling to work one Monday morning, I got a radio message saying go immediately to East Kilbride police station. There they interviewed me about the driver of a taxi I'd just bought, a green Zephyr, EGG 377C. Before telling me anything, they asked about my own whereabouts the night before, where the car should have been parked at the end of the evening shift, and details of who had been driving it. I was very nervous – something serious must have happened to have prompted such a cloak-and-dagger approach.

It *was* very serious. I was informed that my vehicle had been impounded after being involved in a hit-and-run accident in which a cyclist had been killed on the West Mains Road in East Kilbride. He was the father of six children, on his way to work that evening when he was struck by my taxi. I was absolutely gutted.

A fatal accident enquiry followed, but it couldn't establish who had been driving the taxi at the time of the accident. My driver stated that he had parked up for the night and that the car must have been stolen by joyriders.

I'd had no control over events that dreadful night but felt terrible imagining the distress of the dead man's family – how I longed for a magic wand to wave time back. After the accident I cut down to just one vehicle and drove it myself.

I left Z Cars after many disputes with its owner and 'worked the streets' on my own (with no two-way radio). It was at this time that I married for the first time and set up home in East Kilbride in a rented flat. I struggled to pay the rent each month.

After about six months my luck changed when I was given the chance of joining the East Kilbride Taxi Owners Association. I was very happy to remain with them until I was 21 and could join the Glasgow cabs.

I sat my topographical test at the police car pound in Barland Street, Pollokshields when I was 20 and was reprimanded by Sargeant McQuaker of 'the Hackney' for doing so a year early. That was the only time in my life I got into trouble for passing a test! It was my first dealing with 'the Hackney' and I'd earned a reprimand before I even started — must be a record!

Eventually my cab driver's licence came through the post and I received my badge a year later. My number was 3706. Such a high number would make it obvious to other cabbies that I was a rookie, so I never wore my badge. I still keep it safe, in pristine condition.

I drove for my father, in one of his cabs, for three years until I ventured into transport in 1974, still retaining my own vehicle in East Kilbride. A friend and I bought a Scania 80 articulated unit and two trailers but the partnership failed almost immediately and once again I was left holding the baby. I drove the artic myself for a couple of years and ran my taxi at the same time.

The transport business was run from David Street in Bridgeton.

Then I started another driver on the waggon, this time a real good friend who'd been laid off by another transport company. He is George McAteer. He was my saviour. He taught me how to go through life without hassle. I have very few friends I'd call really good friends, but George is definitely there. We became partners for a couple of years before deciding to leave the transport business to the big boys. Then I slipped easily back into the fast blacks.

A natural extension of the cab business, and one I'd stuck to regularly, is the wedding car business, so in 1980 I bought a white Mercedes and, with another good friend, Dick Brown, started a wedding car company which we called White Ribbon Wedding Cars. Dick also bought a white Mercedes and, though the business was small, it proved very popular.

The wedding car fleet at its height

By this time I'd bought my first home, in Mossneuk, East Kilbride – a three-bedroom detached house costing a massive £16,000. I could now say business was looking good. I was off the bottom rung of the ladder. I was running a fleet of seven cabs, three of them brand new, bought from the taxi agent John Paton & Son of Maryhill Road.

My marriage went through turbulent times but we managed to get it back together and moved to a four-bedroom detached house with a magical double garage. Just the job for my wee fleet.

Things ran smoothly in the cab trade until the perfidious Margaret Thatcher spoke those devastating words 'unlimited private hire'. Objections from the taxi trade throughout Britain were to no avail and legislation was railroaded through. I decided that my days as a fleet owner were at an end. I sold all my cabs and bought a mini-market but soon learned there was more to running a shop than I'd thought. I just wasn't cut out to be open all hours.

So I sold the shop and bought three Rolls-Royce Silver Shadows and another Mercedes from a wedding car company that was selling out. With the Mercedes I was already running, I once more owned a small fleet. I organised wedding exhibitions in a dozen hotels to stir up business. Soon the cars were busy most weekends.

I needed premises where I could keep all the vehicles under one roof and managed to find a refurbished railway arch in Commerce Street, near Glasgow City Centre. To offset the cost of the rent and rates I bought a 49-seater coach.

Work for the coach came in fast and furiously so I soon acquired a second one. Though coaches seemed a natural progression from the cab trade, I found this a completely new ball game. To cut a long story short, the coaches were a disaster.

As I was beginning to work this out my marriage broke down completely and I found myself in World War Three. I had to sell my lovely detached house with its double garage and move into a smaller place with my three sons.

On the day we were due to collect the keys for our new home I was told there was a problem — no title deeds were available for the house I was buying. The four of us were homeless. Before the problem was sorted out we spent three weeks at my father-in-law's, pretty bizarre really.

I was now the head of a one-parent family, looking after boys aged 17, 14 and 4. Being a driver and at the same time running a hands-on business was exceptionally demanding, but doing it all from the wreck of a twenty-year marriage blew my mind. Everything to do with the coaches was going wrong. I grappled with vandalism, theft and a coach fire in addition to all the daily problems. For the sake of my sanity I decided I needed a holiday. Maybe my luck would change after that.

After two days in Spain I was just starting to relax when, phoning home, I was told by my middle son Gordon that one of my coaches, driven by Robert Lockhead, had failed to negotiate a bad bend at London Road and had ploughed through a fence and down an embankment, smashing into a telegraph pole. Robert had received severe head and facial injuries. He was dead.

All hell had broken out at home; I had to return immediately. Waiting for my emergency flight, I telephoned again. There was more bad news. The second coach had been repossessed by the hire purchase company as I was a month late with a payment due to a mix-up in the paperwork. There was no earthly need for the repossession – I'd placed a £26,000 deposit on the coach at the time of purchase. I later learned it had been 'repossessed to order'.

I tried to turn my luck around but carrying on proved pointless. The wedding cars held their own but suffered from the financial drain of the coaches. Their number was being steadily depleted in an effort to keep the business afloat. It was time to get out.

My luck and financial resources had dried up. At the age of 40 I was back where I was when just 18 – on the bottom rung of the ladder. My house was first remortgaged then sold to my son – there were more debts to pay than I'd anticipated. It was the most horrendous period of my life, but I still had my health and my boys. With nothing to do and nowhere to go I still had my driver's licence and my sanity.

I went back to the taxi school and resat my knowledge test. When I received my Glasgow Taxi licence I started to drive that very night. I was back (again).

I have now been driving taxis in the Glasgow area for 34 years.

My second son Gordon, who helped me through the dark years, has his own cab in Glasgow. He's the third generation of taxi drivers in our family. He's married and has a little girl called Holly.

My eldest son Stuart, also married and with two sons, Joel and Rhys, is a musician and head music teacher.

Barry, my youngest, has successfully gained a computing degree and moved to Thailand.

I'm remarried to a lovely lady, Irene, and with the grace of God we'll avoid the volcanic days of my past.

It's all too easy to look back and wallow in self pity. In fact I'm very lucky to be where I am.

THE GLASGOW PEOPLE

Glasgow is my city. I have always lived and worked here, or just outside it in East Kilbride. I'm still surrounded by neighbours originally from the city who were re-housed in the days of the Glasgow overspill. As the son of two Glaswegian parents brought up on taxi drivers' tales I must be in as good a position as anyone to give my views on the Glasgow people.

Glasgow's a big city, with a population of about 579,000, and like any other city has its share of hooligans, hardmen and layabouts, but to put all its population into one category would of course be wrong.

I can remember working-class families in the 1950s who were lifelines for poorer families in need, offering food and kindness and any help they could. The Glasgow camaraderie then was very strong indeed. It was probably a roll-over from the war years.

Some of this loyalty to others remains even today. The hearty handshake for friends and strangers alike, a gift of money to a young bairn are still common sights.
It was after the war that Glasgow was branded a violent city, in particular the old Gorbals slums, infamous the world over for street crime and gang warfare.

Time moves on and people with it, but the bitter, often violent rivalry of Celtic and Rangers supporters today all too often boils over into sectarian hatred between Protestants and Catholics. The truth is that these religious groups are an ever-decreasing minority. Most people haven't been inside a church for years, though they can boast about having been season-ticket holders at their clubs since time began. There's a sort of tribal behaviour on both sides when they get together. Mutual hatred still runs very deep. But when the groups are dispersed individuals play down their involvement and common sense returns.

Heavy industry, in particular shipbuilding, steel, and car and truck manufacture, have all left Glasgow, to the cost of Scotland as a whole. Redundancy was a reality for far too many Glasgow people, and the rest felt the knock-on effects. It's not been easy, it's taken longer than expected, but Glasgow is becoming stronger year by year. People have bounced back. Many new businesses have come to Glasgow.

Tourists from all over the world praise the friendliness and unselfishness of the Glaswegian man in the street. I have always worked with Glasgow people and have also been touched by their honesty and generosity.

East Enders have always been a bit different from the rest of Glasgow's people. They're more blunt, more ready to complain, perhaps because in times past the East End was more poverty stricken than the more affluent West End. But ask any cabbie and he'll tell you the same thing. When an East Ender has a few bob in his pocket he'll share it out – even the cabbie gets a good bung. Not like the tight-fisted millionaire in the suburbs who, nine times out of ten, simply thanks you very much and bids you goodnight.

Glasgow people are the friendliest you could ever meet. They have enormous heart for all genuine people and people in need. If you're looking for a friendly city, look no further.

Did you know that the streets in Glasgow are numbered from the centre of the City (Glasgow Cross at the time) outwards, with odd numbers on the left and even numbers on the right? This is helpful to taxi drivers. If a customer asks for, say, 1100 Dumbarton Road you can assume that 1100 is at the far end, near Scotstoun or Yoker. Number 500 would be about halfway along, at Partick.

PICK-UPS AND PUT-DOWNS

The Stories, the Humour, the Patter, the Jokers and the Glasgow People

In a lifetime of driving a cab through the streets of Glasgow I've had many experiences, some pleasant, some unpleasant – the terrifying and the hilarious. Many have enriched my life. All have taught me something. These experiences I would like to share with you.

THE IRN-BRU BOTTLE

Scotland is the only developed country in the world where the number one soft drink is not Coca-Cola. It's well known to all Glaswegians that the second national drink is the famous Barr's Irn-Bru. Every newsagent's shop worth its salt sells it.

It's a miracle cure for that most dreaded of ailments, the self-inflicted monstrous thirst that comes after a real good bevy the night before. Billy Connolly pays homage to this national institution, thanking Mr and Mrs Barr for saving his life on so many Sunday mornings. Almost every Glaswegian has consumed the stuff by the gallon. Never a day goes by but you see people all over carrying cans and bottles of the magic liquid.

Or see an Irn-Bru Taxi passing by....

Taxi drivers are no exception. Only they can't actually carry it so they need a safe place for their bottle where it won't roll about and explode when opened. Its perfect home is the left-hand corner of the driver's cab, between the glass partition and the taxi meter. It will happily hang upside down in the corner, trapped in the triangular space. This cavity was surely designed for this bottle.

The Irn-Bru bottle positioned behind the taxi meter

For years no one paid any attention to a bottle of Irn-Bru sitting there. It was just the obvious place for every cabbie to put his bottle. No problem.

Until a misguided newspaper reported that a driver wishing to make his meter 'go faster' would slip an Irn-Bru bottle upside down

16

into this triangular space so that it rested on the meter. To this day I cannot believe the absolute mayhem this observation caused.

How grown adults could think a glass bottle wedged against the meter could make it go faster was beyond me. Suddenly the little children of punters were whispering, 'The driver's got an Irn-Bru bottle at the meter.'

At first I, like every driver, tried to explain nicely that the comments in the paper were rubbish. Most people accepted the argument that if they had been true the licensing body would withdraw my licence and I'd be charged with fraud. It would be more than my job was worth.

In fact, it would have been easier if we'd withdrawn the Irn-Bru bottles, but this would have created three problems.

(1) There was nowhere else in the cab to put a bottle, that was why we put there in the first place.

(2) We needed to justify ourselves to the public and stop false accusations. Everyone had to accept that the bottle contained a soft drink not a sophisticated computer capable of manipulating the mechanical drive from gearbox to meter. Removing the bottle would be an admission of guilt.

(3) Sheer bloodymindedness.

Some drivers told their passengers it was the intelligence in the Irn-Bru itself that made the meter go faster. If the bottle contained lemonade then the meter would slow down.

Some even believed that one.

At the end of the day it didn't matter what was said, the problem simply wasn't going away.

Some time later I picked up two lads and their girlfriends going to a party. The bright spark sat in one of the bucket seats behind me and started showing off.

'How long have you been driving taxis then, driver?' he yelled in my left ear.

I gave a kind reply and awaited his next attack.

'Earning good money at this job?' he asked sarcastically.

I explaining it was all down to the hours worked, drivers willing to work long hours made a decent enough wage. Knowing this was the build-up to something he'd planned earlier, I slipped in a little dig of my own, 'Sometimes the work's very quiet and the money's poor – so we depend on the big tippers like yourself.'

It drew a laugh from all except him. Anxious to regain his dominance, he retorted, 'Well, my uncle's a taxi driver and I know the score, so you can remove that Irn-Bru bottle from the meter.'

It went quiet in the back of the cab as the tone of the evening dipped below the jovial. This was what he'd been aiming at all along. He'd given his best shot.

'Tell me,' I replied in an understanding tone, 'how does your uncle know I have an Irn-Bru bottle at the meter?'

Again the rear of the cab erupted in three peals of laughter.

'Remove the Irn-Bru bottle,' he demanded.

'I'll remove the bottle if you give me one good reason for it.'

'Because it makes the meter go faster,' he shouted arrogantly.

It was quiet in the back, the tension could be felt by all.

I burst into the loudest Oscar-winning laugh I could create, as if I'd just heard this nonsense for the first time. The more I laughed, the more three of my passengers joined in. I played to the crowd.

'Tell me, how does the Irn-Bru get out of the bottle, into the meter and back again without me seeing it?'

'Stop! There's a police car over there,' he shouted. 'Pull over and they can sort it out.'

I stopped and let him explain the situation to the officer – he attempted to burst some bloodvessels in the process. The friendly bobby chuckled and suggested he carry on his way.

'Just drive then, driver, and go immediately to …' – he gave me the address.

'No, my friend,' I said in disgust, 'this is where you get off. You deserve to walk. It's a nice evening so, when you pass that shop on your way to the party, buy yourself an Irn-Bru for company.'

The other three completed the journey. It felt great leaving him standing by the police car. It made my day.

THE FLYING SQUAD

When I was a young lad, TV programmes about the police fascinated me. 'Dixon of Dock Green' was the first I remember, and 'The Blue Lamp' rekindles a few memories. Hard on its heels came 'Scotland Yard', the first series I recall with the glamorous Flying Squad and high-speed car chases. Those were the days before sirens, when police cars had bells like fire engines.

Ahhh! Riveting stuff ...

I thought I'd never get the chance to drive like the flying squad – speeding through red lights, driving on the wrong side of the road to avoid collisions, sending pedestrians scuttling for the pavements ... Until, that is, I joined the Glasgow Taxis when I was 21.

When I got to drive one of my father's cabs it was fitted with two-way radio so that customers' requirements could be sent from office to taxi – 'over the air' was the term used. This was a whole new world for me.

Unfamiliar phrases had to be learned. The controller would ask for 'a car on the Outpost', then 'a car on the Cunningham Street rank'. The old Buchanan Bus Station had a 'taxi rank' opposite which

The old Royal Maternity Hospital in Rottenrow

was for one solitary car only – hence the nickname 'the Outpost'. If no car answered the call for the Outpost it was the turn of the feeder rank to receive the call. The feeder rank was in Cunningham Street and here cars waited their turn for the Outpost.

Another frequent call was for 'the Flying Squad at the Mat'. The Mat was the old Royal Maternity Hospital in Rottenrow and the Flying Squad was just that – a police escort by one of the fastest suped-up police cars with the now familiar go-faster stripes.

This sounded pretty glamorous to me and I waited expectantly for some time before I was lucky enough to be the nearest car to the Mat. Then it was my turn …

Every car had its own call sign – mine was Victor 3. The controller announced: 'Victor 3. Emergency job at the Mat for doctors and nurses going to Blackhill. Wait for the Flying Squad if they are not at the Mat when you pick up the staff.'

When I arrived at Rottenrow two doctors, two nurses and an infant respirator were loaded into my cab, the Flying Squad arriving as I was just about ready to roll. A young policeman in a brand new Triumph 2000 pulled up alongside and said he'd be leading me to Govanhill. When he approached a set of traffic lights he'd stop the traffic so that as I reached the junction I could drive straight through. At this point he'd charge on to the next set of lights and do the same there.

I was ready and willing but questioned the destination. I'd been told Blackhill not Govanhill. He was sure he was right so we were off without delay.

My old 2.2 diesel was heavily loaded and I soon realised I was going to struggle to keep up with this supercharged Triumph. At almost the first junction I was under pressure.

My uniformed friend did exactly as he'd said. Motorists always respect white police cars with flashing blue lights and gaudy red stripes. Everyone stopped and the junction cleared instantly.

But no one respects a black cab. For a start they'd think it was just trying to pull a fast one, following the police car to get through the traffic quicker. I screamed silently as I sped through the junction, hoping no smarty pants drivers on the front line were riding their clutches, trying to cut me off.

At every junction the feeling was the same. I flew through red light after red light and at every one I was on the wrong side of the road. I soon began to question the glamorous image of the Flying Squad – I was absolutely terrified.

If anyone crossed in front of me I could be dead. If not that, I dreaded my father's reaction when I told him I'd been involved in an accident, bearing in mind several hundred lectures about 21-year-olds and cabs. My heart raced furiously. My right foot pressed hard on the accelerator as I struggled to catch up with my leader.

We were soon approaching Govanhill – as far as I was concerned it could not come soon enough. My job was almost over as we entered Govanhill Street. Arriving at the close, my cab doors burst open and doctors and nurses flew upstairs, carrying their heavy machinery like an empty carton.

The police driver came over and asked me how I was feeling. My language was choice at the beginning. I assured him I'd soon be back to normal but if I never did another Flying Squad job ever again I'd be delighted. He laughed at me as he could clearly see I was shaken up.

Suddenly the medical party came rushing out of the close with the machine. 'You're right, driver,' said the doctor, 'it's Hogganfield Street in Blackhill, not Govanhill.'

I nearly laid an egg.

We were off again, same routine as before, red light after red light, weaving in and out of traffic jams, almost driving on the pavement. The weather had changed for the worse and we found ourselves in thick fog. I prayed that the other drivers would see me at the junctions. The doctors were throwing in their tuppence-worth – how long before we reached Blackhill? I must have told them six times in five minutes.

Pressure was also on them, they knew every minute lost would lessen their chance of saving the baby's life. They were getting reports from the hospital – the situation was critical.

At Blackhill they went through the same routine as before. There was nothing left for me to do but try to calm my nerves. The police driver went to another incident and I was on my own.

An ambulance arrived after several minutes, its driver was complaining about thick fog: 'I couldn't see a finger in front of me! It's bad, isn't it?'

I was too shaken up to reply – my only concern was to stop my heart from bursting. I was tensed behind the wheel, my eyes closed, trying to calm down, when one of the doctors approached. He handed me a test tube and told me it was a specimen taken from the newly delivered child – which I was please to take to the maternity hospital with the utmost urgency. They were waiting for me. It was a matter of life and death that I get there as soon as I possibly could. Next thing I remember is being on the road again, battling to make speed through a pea-soup fog, and no help from the Flying Squad.

Other motorists were driving very cautiously, unprepared for the approach of this mad racing taxi driver flashing his lights, trying to overtake. This journey was worse even than Govanhill and Blackhill.

At the Mat the test tube was welcomed by anxious staff and my job was at last over. My nerves were in such a state I was forced to go home for a few hours to recover.

Later I worked out my job price and found it to be the princely sum of £4/10/-. No great reward for a near-coronary.

This was my first and last Flying Squad job.

THE SILENT CUSTOMER

It's amazing how often this happens. A lady gets into the cab, settles herself on the rear seat and says nothing.

She's obviously deep in thought.

So the driver asks politely, 'Where'd you like to go, my dear?'

As if surprised by his ignorance, she'll say, 'My mother's.'

THE BEST ONE-LINER – EVER!

During a week of torrential rainfall there was flooding all over Glasgow and the road network had its fair share.

Favourite places to flood are always roads under railway bridges, which dip down to give extra height for buses and trucks to pass through. In very wet weather it's all too common to see vehicles stranded in floodwaters under bridges.

In Springburn there was a very bad flood near the junction of Royston Road, where the old Red Hackle railway bridge used to be. A double-decker corporation bus was brought to a sudden stop as it tried to plough its way through to the other side of the bridge. The depth of the water was several feet, high enough to enter the engine compartment.

The passengers were evacuated and shortly afterwards the water level rose until it submerged the windows on the lower deck.

About this time Charles Reid came scooting along in his taxi, totally oblivious to the problem of the newly formed lake. Hitting the floodwaters, he made no attempt to apply his brakes or attempt to swerve. The cab made gracious headway into the pool, sending a massive wave to slam into the half-submerged bus, and was instantly swallowed up.

It was totally submerged except for the white flag on the roof, fluttering freely on the radio aerial which was sticking out a few inches above the water. The driver had escaped from the cab by swimming and now stood at the poolside, completely drookit.

It took him a few moments to come to terms with what had just happened, then he was in a state of total shock and disbelief at what he'd done.

He was approached by a fellow cab driver who'd come to help. Anxious to keep the situation low key, the friend was nevertheless very keen to find out how Charlie had managed to drown his taxi.

'What were you thinking of to drive into the floodwater like that?'
The reply was epic: 'I thought the bus was a single decker!'

THE SHORTEST ROUTE

Every taxi driver I know sets out each day with the best of intentions to earn a good wage, look after his cab and serve the public. But coping with punters and dealing with traffic and other frustrations is not easy. Pressure affects every driver differently.

We have to deal with people who are late for work or who've just had a run-in with the boss and who use us as prime targets

to vent their frustrations. We have to cope with drunks, junkies, football hooligans and the ever-growing number of numpties out there. Every night there're stag parties spilling rowdy guys onto the streets, shouting and swearing, thinking they're the bee's knees as comedians and that everyone finds them the cleverest thing since sliced bread. Sometimes they take a few cabs from one pub to another as they trundle along their merry way to total oblivion.

'Follow that cab!' I wish I had a tenner for every loud-mouthed idiot who thought that was original. Experience teaches you that the best way to deal with the remark is to laugh as if you've just heard it for the first time – that way everyone is happy.

The most common bone of contention between passenger and driver is the route. There are many reasons for this. Unfortunately they can't all be solved.

The shortest distance between any two points is a straight line.

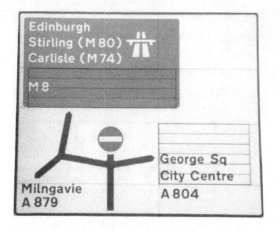

Now, although this is perfectly true, it is unhelpful. So it's in the driver's discretion to take the route he thinks will make the journey most cost-effective. This is not necessarily the shortest route. It's not even always the quickest route.

I'll explain.

The shortest route may take driver through the City Centre or through roadworks. Both could result in delays or even gridlock and so incur waiting-time penalties, as of course the taxi meter records both distance and time.

The quickest route may involve driving along a motorway for several miles then doubling back to the drop-off point. A four-mile journey could become six miles and the additional two miles would have to be paid for by the customer though the time gain was only a minute.

Every journey needs the driver to make a sensible decision as to the route. The customer may travel the same journey every day and therefore know the best way to go to avoid delays. Unfortunately the taxi driver doesn't know where his fare is going until he's inside the cab, and then he has only a second or two to decide in which direction to set off. If his initial decision is wrong, the customer will think he doesn't know where he's going or that he's 'taking the tourist route'. The poor driver then has to dig himself out of a hole.

Which brings me to words every Glasgow taxi driver dreads:

'Yur gawin' the rang wie!'

Or, 'Whit wie ur yi gawin'?'

It stops you dead in your tracks. Many punters really don't know the quickest way home. They're used to the bus route and because they go that way every evening feel sure it's the shortest way. Most don't ask politely which route you're about to take or give you the benefit of the doubt. I always wonder what jobs they do, which industry employs them that they're so perfect as never to make mistakes themselves, or so suppressed by a boss yelling at them that they do likewise to someone else at the first opportunity.

I always repeat the name of the street a customer gives me, adding the area of Glasgow it's in. This confirms I'm about to go to the right location, and the area it's in is added confirmation. That way, if we get to the address and it's not the one they want I can say that I checked both address and area.

I picked up one gent in the City Centre who, through deep inebriation, told me he was going to what sounded like 'Boydstone Road'. This I repeated and he confirmed it.

'Boydstone Road in Carnwadric?'

Again he agreed.

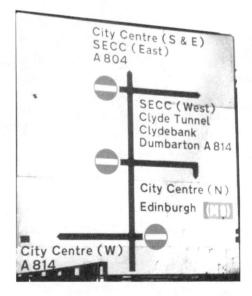

We travelled due south to Boydstone Road, about five miles from where I'd picked him up.

A voice piped up from the rear, 'Where the f**k are we?'

'Exactly where you asked to go, Boydstone Road.'

'Naw, naw, naw! Ah didnae say that. Ah said Royston Road.'

What if anything goes on in a head like that? I've just spent twenty minutes travelling south for five miles –

26

surely if he stayed three miles to the north-east (an eight-minute journey) some alarm bells should have started ringing? Obviously not.

Now, who is to blame for this error? I leave the decision to you.

After some heated words I drove him to Royston Road ... he would only have given the next taxi driver an earful. But all the way I fumed at the thought I wouldn't get paid for the extra journey. On a straight run from the city to Royston Road I'd have about £4 on my meter. As it was I'd switched the meter off, but I estimated the total fare for the journey I'd done would have been £15.

I asked him for £4. I gritted my teeth as he handed me a fiver and waited for his change.

Ah, to serve the public is a wonderful thing. You can't win 'em all.

Every customer has his or her own reason for wanting to travel a particular way. Say, for instance, I think the best way to complete a journey is along the motorway but the difference in price for travelling the alternative route is minimal – then I'll offer the customer the choice.

One will say, 'Oh, definitely take the motorway.' Another will opt for the other route. The driver doesn't need to know their reasons, he just likes happy customers.

One may volunteer the information that she likes this route because her grandmother's house is on the road and she can confirm everything looks in order as she passes her door. I've even had it said to me by one lady passenger that she wanted to pass her husband's ex-girlfriend's house to make sure his car wasn't parked outside!

We all have our reasons for preferring this way to that, but bear in mind that the driver has views of his own about your journey. With the best of intentions I think I'm going the sensible way, only to have a good lady from Knightswood suggest I'm nothing but a bloodsucker.

She wanted to go from Dumbarton Road, Whiteinch to Fulton Street. I repeated the address: Fulton Street, Anniesland. Yes. Off we went.

Turning into Fulton Street, I asked where to stop. She indicated the other end of the street, which is about a mile long. There she told me to pull up outside her house. After paying the fare she bitterly complained about the route I'd taken: the quicker way would have been along Dumbarton Road and up Lincoln Avenue. She was actually quite correct, but when I'd repeated the address I'd confirmed that the area was Anniesland. Her end of the street was in Knightswood. How is any driver to know which end of the street his passenger wants if he's not told?

Now Glasgow people aren't known for being shy. Which brings me to my next point about taking the tourist route. Every driver makes mistakes and I wouldn't suggest I've never taken the wrong route, but if I don't notice the blunder myself I'm usually jerked into a rethink by my passenger.

It may be that in many parts in Britain taxi drivers are able to take advantage of their public and stretch out journeys for their own benefit, but I can assure you Glasgow is not one of them. The Glasgow public are no fools, they don't stand for that kind of nonsense. Any potential taxi drivers out there thinking Glasgow punters might be an easy target had better think again. Remember the old comedians who died a death in Glasgow's theatres – the Alhambra, the Empire, the old Metropole…? Ask them about the Glasgow public's reaction when they think you're trying to get one over on them.

Did you know that the word 'hackney' comes from the French *hacquenée* meaning strong horse? Just the horse itself was originally available for journeys; later it was harnessed to a vehicle known as a *Coche à Hacquenée*. In 1834 the hansom cab was patented by Joesph Aloysius Hansom. In those days a law was passed to allow the driver of the cab to stay with his horses: it granted him permission to urinate at the front wheel of his carriage without prosecution. The hansom cab was the most popular carriage until the motorised cab arrived in the early twentieth century.

TWO DRUNK LADIES AT GLASGOW CROSS

I picked up a drunk woman at the taxi rank at Glasgow Cross. The passenger door had been opened by her companion before I realised just how drunk she was.

Only one of the women wanted to travel, the other was keen to be off again to the tavern across the road to fulfil her heart's desire of becomeing absolutely paralytic. In such circumstances the best thing for a driver is to pull away and leave the hire standing, but as my door was being held open escape was impossible.

'Cum own, Jessie,' the considerate friend encouraged, 'Cum own, get yur arse in here. The driver's no' got awe day. Cum own. Cum own.'

Jessie was attempting to stagger across the pavement to the cab but, as her friend was holding the door open, she had no support and was banging her head against the taxi pole at the front of the rank and bumping into the open door. At last she tripped over the taxi step and fell inside safely.

'Oh driver,' called the loyal companion, 'yi'll need ti excuse her, she speeks wi' a stammer.'

THE PARKWAY BAR STOOLS

One summer's evening about 8 o'cock I was flagged down by a young woman of about 30 outside the Parkway Tavern on Paisley Road West, in Cardonald. She was carrying a large bag and also transporting two stools. She wasn't going far, just down the road to Govan. When we arrived she admitted she had no money to pay the £2.50 fare.

She emptied the contents of her bag onto the back seat and I was surprised to see twenty or thirty deodorant sprays.

'I'm a shoplifter,' she explained. 'You can have six deodorants, that will be worth more to you than the money.'

'I don't want your deodorants, I want the money.'

'Up to you driver – I'm absolutely skint. You can have six deodorants or the two bar stools I just knocked from the Parkway Tavern.'

The Parkway Tavern on Paisley Road West

COWS

Working in the radio room one day, I heard a driver 'blow in' to the controller, suggesting he let other cabs know that animals were running along the East Kilbride to Glasgow road. Having just escaped from a field, they were in full flight.

In the interests of safety, the controller repeated the message, warning of cows on the East Kilbride-Glasgow road.

Sharp as a razor, one young wag of a driver replied, 'Do we know any of them?'

YOU CAN'T GET IN THAT SIDE

The summer brings long waits for drivers, especially on a rank the trade describes as 'not working'. To cut the boredom they'll joke and tell stories.

It was one of those days absolutely nothing was happening. Time was running very slowly when eventually it was my turn to be first on the rank.

It wasn't elation that I felt when approached by the local drunk who'd just vacated his local, brimming with liquid refreshment. He entered the cab through the offside door, 'the suicide door', and started to apologise for the very short journey he wanted to make.

I interrupted before he could give the address: he couldn't enter from the wrong side, he'd need to get out and walk round to the correct side.

'Sorry! Sorry, driver.' He meekly got out, walked round the front of the cab and re-entered from the pavement side.

It didn't earn me any extra money but it gave me something to talk about when I got back to the rank.

Did you know that the old-style taximeter of the 'fifties and 'sixties was fitted with a 'For Hire' light that looked like a flag? To engage the meter, the flag was pulled down to record the fare.

This was known as 'dropping the flag', as term that has remained in use even though modern electronic meters are operated by pushing a button. The old meter also showed the recommended tip for the driver and this was displayed in a small window beside the recorded fare.

SANDRA'S TOILET

I picked up a lady one day who asked for the public toilets in St Vincent Place, just past George Square. It was just a short journey within the City Centre.

She said her name was Sandra and she'd read a newspaper article the previous evening about a new state-of-the-art disabled toilet at ground level on the same site as the downstairs St Vincent Place toilets.

'It's a big bonus for me,' she confided. 'Not all shops have disabled toilets on the ground floor. Some are downstairs, some upstairs, and with my disability I can't use any of them.'

On arriving she thanked me and paid me off.

Stuck in the traffic, going nowhere, I watched her make her way towards the splendid facility she'd awaited so eagerly. On reaching it, however, she turned away and came straight back to my cab.

There was a notice pinned to the door: 'Toilet open – key downstairs'.

Only in Glasgow…

The disabled toilet between the male and female toilets in St Vincent Place

THE GRIFFIN BAR

An old driver who drove one of my cabs in the early 'seventies was called Willie McCulley, but believe it or not I had two drivers with that name. This one stayed in Scotstoun.

Talking to him one day about the cab trade, he told me that when he started he was quickly disillusioned. He'd expected everyone taking taxis to be well-to-do – people going to the airport, functions, theatres, that sort of thing. He hadn't considered that common people also need to get about.

The King's Theatre in Bath Street

After some weeks driving cabs he still hadn't taken a fare to the airport or any of the theatres. But his luck changed one night when he picked up a well-dressed young gent who asked for 'The King's Theatre'.

The tide must have turned, he thought – the first few weeks were clearly his initiation, now real taxi work was starting to come his way.

Nearing the end of the journey, he asked what performance was playing that evening. More disillusionment followed.

'Oh, I'm not going to the King's,' his passenger replied, 'I'm going to the Griffin bar across the road.'

The Griffin Bar opposite the King's Theatre

GINJUR

Driving cabs all over the city and then being asked to stop in strange places and hang on for passengers, for one reason or another, gives you the chance to look closely at things that would normally fly by.

Sitting outside Barr's soft drinks factory in Parkhead, where they make Scotland's other national drink Irn-Bru (known in true Glasgow slang as Ginjur) I noticed a small Chinese carry-out shop in Springfield Road. It looked nothing more than a hovel, it probably failed even to qualify for the environmental health hit-list. How it had managed to stay open was a mystery. (In fact it closed before I could photograph it in business.)

The Shatin Palace in Springfield Road, Parkhead

Behind the wire-mesh grill over the front window (which hadn't seen Mr Sheen for many a year) was a handwritten sign in pidgin English:

Hame Delivery
Breed   Rolls
Fags
Ginjur

FREE BEER

Passing Spud Milligan's pub in Argyle Street one night with four university student passengers, each an intellectual in his own right, they noticed the permanent sign above the entrance: 'Free beer tomorrow.'

There was a lengthy and intense debate before they came to the conclusion there was bound to be a catch ...

FLAGGED DOWN

We taxi drivers will constantly look for a fare as we travel empty. Often a hire will be standing at a bus stop, so we pay particular attention to these, they can be a constant source of work.

An arm will suddenly shoot out of the shelter at the last moment as you pass. You must then make an instant decision. Check your mirror, brake and try to pull into the bus bay all within a nanosecond. You can feel proud if you achieve this manoeuvre without causing any other driver the inconvenience of having to slow down or swerve round you.

It's then most humiliating to see your would-be passenger march past and hop onto a double-decker bus that's just pulled in behind you. The first idea that springs into your mind is that the bus driver's wetting himself at your humiliation.

Another scenario is where a male punter hails your cab with a full-length, deliberate stretch of the arm and (nanosecond reactions spot on) you swerve safely into the kerb beside him just in time to see him twist his wrist, bend his elbow and check his watch.

Perhaps most annoying of all is to be flagged down only to be asked for directions.

Then there's the classic pick-up in the middle of a traffic jam. Imagine the queue of traffic almost at standstill trying to squeeze through a major set of traffic lights ahead. You've waited patiently for several changes of the lights but the volume of traffic is so heavy that only a couple of cars manage to get through each time.

At last your taxi's in pole position, waiting to turn right. The lights are about to change. You engage first gear for the quick getaway that'll enable a second car to pass through after you.

It's at this point that Mr Numpty appears from nowhere and – guess what? He's looking for a cab.

Time is of the essence but a quick entry by a single guy will be fine. You give him the nod, the hire is 'on'. Then the lights change. You turn round hoping to see him seated in the back but he's holding the door open for his wife. Only she's not quite made it this far yet, she's still on the opposite side of the street.

Your heart sinks, a curse belches out of your mouth automatically. Then the dreaded words:

'Cum own Iza, hurry up!'

'Naw, it isnae safe in the middle eh the street.'

'Cum oan Iza, Ah'm hodin' the f**kin' door fur yi. The driver's waitin' ... the metur's oan.'

'Naw, Ah'm no' crossin' the street wi' this pram!'

Every motorist behind you is cursing you. They're leaning on their horns. No way do you get any sympathy. The passenger door's open and you can't move but horns are screaming all the way back down the queue.

The lights switch back to red and traffic flows in the opposite direction.

'Awe right Iza, the lights huv chinged. There's nothing cumin', cum own,' calls Numpty with relief.

'Awe right, just help mi git the weans inti the motur.'

Neither has an inkling of the mayhem they've caused, they're totally oblivious to the rage from the queue. It's times like this you realise the whole world's against taxi drivers.

Mrs Numpty is now laying into her spouse for harassing her.

We're still in pole position at the lights, me waiting with baited breath to turn right. The passengers in the back settle, there's the click of the door closing, then the sound of Mrs Numpty's voice.

'Okay we're in, driver.'

'Yu'v no' shut the f**kin' door right!' Her husband shows a modicum of impatience. 'Cum own, get oot the wye, Ah'll git it.'

The door opens again, followed swiftly by an almighty bang that rocks the cab.

'That's it this time, driver!'

The next change of lights is only seconds away, you're ready to roll, then the sweet voice of Mr Numpty again:

'Turn left, driver. We're gawin' the other wye.'

The curse could be heard in Los Angeles.

I edge out, cut across the traffic and wave, thanking disbelieving drivers for their patience. I'm on my way, thinking *What a nightmare!* Soon my blood pressure will return to normal.

Then the voice: 'Driver! Stope at the first shope, we need mulk fur the wean.'

THE UNFORGETTABLE NIGHT OUT

Around 1am on a Sunday morning I picked up a dejected reveller heading for home after an evening with his mates. Tripping over the entrance step, he landed with a small thud on the back seat. He started to complain about his ejection from a nightclub.

'My mates got in, driver, but I got a knockback. I mean, I've had a few, I know, but I'm anything but drunk!'

He felt the pain of rejection acutely.

'Why were you knocked back?' I asked.

'The big bouncer thought he was a funny man. He asked me where I'd been before coming there, and all I said was I didn't know.'

THE HANDBAG

A young lady asked to leave the cab to go into her flat for the £8 fare and offered to leave her handbag as security.

When I agreed, she thanked me politely and assured me she'd only be a couple of minutes.

Suspicious after ten minutes, I checked the handbag.

It contained a common builder's brick.

FOXY LADY

When on a radio job, it's a basic requirement for the driver to be given the customer's name. I was put in my place one day when I arrived to pick up a passenger I'd been told was called Fox only to be informed with firm politeness that her correct name was Mrs Christina Fox-Bryce-Lloyd.

BRINGING THE SUBJECT UP

I often get compliments from customers about how clean and fresh-smelling my cab is. Some ask if it's brand new and are surprised to hear it's four years old. Some dwell on the subject that little bit longer by saying it's the cleanest cab they've ever been in.

One or two even comment what a dreadful shame it would be if someone was sick in it.

'Oh, it's really not that bad,' I reply. I go on to inform them that a purpose-built taxicab has been designed with such problems in mind – all the interior surfaces such as seat covers, door panels and roof linings are made with washable materials and can be cleaned quite easily.

Then I like to wind them up a little.

'It's funny you should bring the subject up,' I say. 'Only about an hour ago – my last hire in fact – I picked up an old drunk who threw up in the corner just about where you're sitting.'

I take a good look into the mirror to observe an uncomfortable passenger screw up his face, look behind him and lift his rear end just in case he's sitting on something sticky. It takes only a few seconds for the predictable shift of places: I watch for the sliding motion as he heads for the opposite corner.

Having distanced himself from an unwanted residue of bodily fluids, he starts to relax. But I'm not finished with him.

With a straight face I explain that looking into the rear-view mirror has upset my sense of left and right – I'd made a mistake about which corner I'd cleaned. 'It's actually the one you're in now.'

I get the same reaction as before. He ends up back where he started.

'Clean as a whistle then, isn't it?' I ask.

'Yeah. Excellent.' My companion now observes my face bursting to laugh.

Realising the joke's on him he also starts to laugh and a relieved and happy customer leaves the cab.

THANK YOU FOR NOT SMOKING

It was a radio job. As I pulled up outside the close in Maryhill I noticed the young lad had almost finished his cigarette. He
opened the door but before entering asked if I had any objections
to his smoking in the cab.

As not much of the offending ember was left, I nodded that it
was okay.

He turned round and yelled to his four mates coming downstairs,
all puffing away, 'Alright guys, driver says we can smoke.'

THE LAST LAUGH

Provanmill is an area in the East End of Glasgow. With the M8
motorway running close by, it's one of the more deprived and less
picturesque parts of our city.

One fine evening about 9pm I picked up four youths in their late
teens. I put them in the streetwise bracket, just short of me calling
them something else. Close to where I picked them up stands that
grand old establishment, Barlinnie prison. I felt sure that each in
turn would take up residence in that desirable property for at least
a short spell, if only to obtain the accreditation certificate.

These guys were very boisterous – full of harassment may be a
better description. They asked me to take them into town, but as
you can imagine the party started when they entered the cab. Even
at that stage I didn't much care whether I was going to be paid, I
only wanted them out.

They knew one another well, that much was easy to tell – their
cursing and swearing at each other only brought shouts and extrav-
agant gestures of agreement in similar vocabulary.

Just after leaving the pick-up point we started to cross the motorway. Both rear windows had been fully opened and two jeering
muppets had their bodies half out of the cab, trying to attract the

attention of the locals as I tried to glide unobtrusively along the fly-over. No sooner had I engaged third gear than there was a shriek from a muppet in the back. Stop immediately!

I pointed out that we were in the middle of a flyover and I couldn't stop.

On reaching the other side I was told with a modicum of Glasgow slang I was to get my arse back over the other side, loud mouth had dropped something as he hung out of the window. I did as I was told and came to a halt in no-man's-land. Two guys hopped out of the cab to search, creating more din as they left.

It was a big joke to them but for me about as funny as a trip to the dentist. I waited beside the pavement in the middle of the fly-over with both passenger doors open as the two remaining members of the Broons Family yelled insults at the searching muppets.

New instructions boomed from the rear: 'Drive up an' doon the street, driver, and Ah'll hang oot o' the windae to see if Ah can see it.'

The doors slammed shut. I turned the vehicle round again to avoid further abuse. We crawled along the flyover in a fruitless search, though my two companions could have spotted 5p at a hundred paces.

'Nae joy, Tam?'

'Naw, nae f**kin' joy.'

'Let's get aff 'n' walk over there and the f**kin' driver will jist huvtie wait.'

I couldn't believe all four were leaving the cab – Utopia! 'Take as long as you like, lads!'

Both back doors were left open as they went treasure hunting. I took this as a sign of distrust.

But of course I would wait.

All of three seconds.

Taking off, even with both rear doors open, was liberating.

I was unable to find out what it was they'd been looking for until, several hires later, a young girl let out a scream. 'Driver, there's a set of teeth down there looking at me!'

One of the muppets had been shouting so loud his teeth had fallen out and slipped down inside, not outside, the door, landing in a corner.

The sight of those teeth made all the hassle I'd received feel worthwhile. I had the last laugh.

CHILD'S PLAY

To say that today the safety of children is a top priority would be a great understatement. Every parent and grandparent has good cause for concern when their offspring are away from them for even the shortest of periods.

With this in mind, I became anxious when I failed to make contact with a 10-year-old girl travelling home from a local theatrical event. I was to have picked her up at the front door of the small theatre at a set time in the afternoon and take her home to her mother. Five minutes had elapsed after the pick-up time. My cab was parked right at the front entrance but I had no idea what the child looked like or what she was wearing.

Having failed to make contact inside the theatre, I had no alternative but to inform my radio room of the situation and they in turn rang the child's mother, who had ordered the cab, and this set off a panic reaction.

After fifteen minutes, I'd visited the now familiar interior of the theatre several times without success. Nerves began to strain in me and in the radio-room staff who were in direct contact with the frantic mother.

Eventually the controller began to question my location. Was I at the theatre's main front door? For a split second I thought I'd blown it, that I'd created all this commotion because I'd gone to the wrong door. But one more glance at the building and I could assure him that I was only a few feet from the main, the only entrance to the theatre.

There was a pause, then the controller came back to me saying he'd just had the girl on her mobile phone stating clearly that she was at the exit to the theatre and there was definitely no sign of me. At least we'd established she was safe. We could now go about the business of getting her picked up.

I'd noticed a young girl standing about twenty feet away from my cab but she was so close to me, and had seen my cab arriving and watched me sitting there for the last twenty minutes, that I'd assumed she wasn't waiting for me. I'd left my vehicle several times, run up and down the theatre steps and she'd definitely seen me – I had to pass her on my way to the theatre. Surely this couldn't be the child everyone was frantic about?

To remove any doubt that I had, I approached her. Was she was so-and-so, the young lady to be picked up in a taxi?

'Oh yes,' she said 'that's my name. I've been waiting twenty minutes.'

Cautiously, trying not to startle her with my surprise at her not coming forward, I asked if she was feeling well, and hadn't she noticed there'd been a bright purple-and-yellow taxi cab waiting at the front door of the theatre for rather a long time, and that the driver was in and out of it many times looking for someone?

'Oh yes,' she agreed. 'But my mother said I wasn't to get into any taxi except a black cab.'

STUDENTS

Glasgow's colleges and universities are famous and respected throughout the world. Their high standards attract students from all over Britain and the Continent to Glasgow.

And the taxi trade is grateful for the business these students bring. All drivers know how important this is so we're always student friendly, even when our patience is pushed to the limit.

Most of the journeys students undertake are short, mainly around the West End and City Centre, but at weekends these small journeys can contribute a sizeable amount to the income of a cabbie.

Glasgow University

A regular occurrence every driver experiences is students trying to divide a £4 fare between five travellers. They'll consult each other earnestly and, even without a calculator, eventually, in the fullness of time, manage to come up with the correct answer.

There then follows a debate about what proportion of the fare each student can afford to pay. All this as you sit impatiently waiting for payment from our future lawyers and doctors.

What chance is there for the rest of us, you think, if the cream of our intelligentsia find it this difficult to divide 4 by 5?

Jimmy has only 63p.

Philip has even less.

Roberta (studying law) has the exact fare required to fulfil her contractual obligations.

Gillian needs the autobank (back at the pick-up point).

Mary has enough to cover her own share, with a few pence left towards the shortfall of the rest. She takes time to explain that the return of this money by 9am next morning is required as her unexpected overspend is required for a luncheon.

You're missing work over all this.

'It's time to pay the driver, guys,' instructs Gillian, who has no cash at all. 'Dig deep everyone, the driver's waiting.'

This is clearly code for everyone search your pockets. Every pocket is raked several times

Glasgow Caledonian University

until eventually £4 can be made up. Handing over a large handful of smash totalling the exact fare, not a penny more, five happy passengers, oblivious to the time they've cost you, thank you nicely and trot off innocently to the campus to continue their hilarities.

Is it surprising that we look forward to the summer holidays?

But, hey, what we'd give to turn the clock back!

Did you know that a Glasgow taxi driver plying for hire on a taxi rank must take you to your desired destination within the Glasgow city boundary unless he has a valid reason to refuse?

THE ORANGE WALK

The Saturday before July 12th is when the Orange Order in Glasgow turn out for their annual parade. It's a time of great merriment. Each Orange lodge is represented, each with its own brightly coloured uniform, mostly blue or orange, representing the Protestant religion and their hero, William of Orange, 'King Billy'. At the Battle of the Boyne in 1690 he won victory for the Protestants in Ireland, defeating the Catholic King James VII.

They carry huge banners and most have their own bands – there are Highland Bands, Brass Bands and Accordion Bands, but most striking of all are the Orange Flute Bands.

They march from every corner of the city to an outdoor meeting in one of Glasgow's public parks. There's a religious service and speeches, then something to eat, usually accompanied by some liquid refreshment. For many it's the best day of the year.

The King William III Monument now stands in Cathedral Square

Standing at the roadside as the march trundles past is an experience you can't forget. The dancing, the swaying of the banners and the sounds of the bands are unique to the Orange Walk.

By about 6 o'clock, when the bands eventually get back to their own areas, they're exhausted, but life seeps back on the home straight as family and friends give them a rousing finale. The hard work over, what better place to rest their weary legs, quench their thirst, and reminisce, than the pub?

Not everyone sees this event in the same joyous light of course. To Glasgow's Catholics it's an insult, rousing a sense of anger that their humiliation over three hundred years ago should be celebrated today.

One Saturday, July 12th 1973, the day of the Orange Walk, I was working night shift. I'd made an agreement with myself that, at the first sign of trouble, I'd pull over for a break until the pubs were out and the city was quiet.

It was 10pm. In those days Glasgow's barbaric licensing laws meant that the pubs now had to stop serving. Because they closed so early, customers would wash down as much alcohol as possible in the last half-hour before the final bell, and order extra rounds. When the bell went at 10pm the amount of drink on most tables was vast and the licensing laws dictated that it all be consumed in the ten-minute drinking-up period. When tanked-up customers spilled out of the pubs at 10.15 into the fresh air many became instantly paralytic.

Such was the case this particular Saturday. I'd pulled onto the Govan Cross rank to service a small queue from local hostelries and a young gent and two fine ladies climbed into my cab. Full of merriment from the day's events, he knelt on the floor behind me, pulled the bucket seat down onto his knees and started banging it like a drum from his Orange band.

Singing an Orange Anthem, 'The Sash', he instructed me to 'Just drive!'

I politely asked him where he wanted to go.

'Just f**kin' drive!'

The Govan Cross taxi rank

At 21 years of age I could handle myself and did not feel intimidated. I told him to leave the cab, I wasn't taking him anywhere. To my relief he and his two ladies departed without a word.

By this time the queue at the rank was swelling. Unfortunately for me, at the head of it was a middle-aged gent definitely the worse for wear. He clutched the taxi-rank pole for support and reached out for my door handle at the same time. After several swipes had fallen a couple of feet short I thought I'd better get out and help the poor soul inside. Big mistake.

He thanked me for helping him in.

Walking round the back of the cab I came face to face with the young gent I'd ejected only minutes before.

Did I think I was smart bringing him down in front of his lady friends? Before I could answer, he threatened to 'burst' me. A delightful Glasgow expression informing me he was going to smash my face.

He was clearly not going to be appeased. I was given another warning about the unsuitability of my facial features. Such a second warning at 10.20pm in the middle of Govan Cross it is unwise to ignore. A second before he struck out at me I decided attack was the best form of defence and sent a right-handed volley into the middle of his face. World War Three had begun.

Rolling in the street, exchanging blows, we were joined by his ladies. The punching, the kicking and the scratching was punctuated by curses until we were at last pulled apart by the ever-swelling taxi queue.

I made it back to the safety of my cab but, on closing the door, was confronted by an open barber's razor which seemed to appear from nowhere through my open window. Reacting instinctively, I retreated from the driver's seat to the space beneath the taxi meter on the left-hand side of the cab. The long arm of the razor-slasher was furiously reaching in towards my face. Side to side, the razor cut the air only an inch away.

My attacker was eventually pulled away and I frantically clambered into the driver's seat. As I was locking my door and window the rear door burst open and an intruder tried to grab me from behind. This time I had the advantage. I managed to shut the sliding partition window, but only a second had separated me from a nasty fate.

The left front door then burst open and another intruder bundled in, swinging his fists, as I tried to make an emergency call to my controller. The radio microphone was wrenched from its socket and the battle continued. The controller, having received only half of my emergency call, was sending all available taxis to the Govan Lyceum, a bingo hall half a mile away. I could expect no help from any of my comrades.

After several blows my attacker fled, leaving the door open. I

pulled the cord which would normally close it ... but, due to the recent Irn-Bru controversy, I'd moved the bottle from its usual slot to the retaining door-strap cavity and it had become wedged in the door gap so that it was impossible to close the door. It took only seconds to remove the bottle but it seemed like forever.

Now the driver's door and front luggage door were both secured and the intruder in the back couldn't figure out that the partition window operated on a slide not an up-and-down movement. I was congratulating myself that I'd soon be safely out of there.

Regaining control as I climbed into the driver's seat, I looked out of the windscreen in time to see another male fire a full beer can at me. Smashing into the windscreen, it burst open and beer poured down the window. Undeterred, he let a second beer can fly and I couldn't believe my luck when that also burst open. But, as I engaged first gear and hit the beer-can artist, I paused for a split second and saw an army of youths running at me from the other side of Govan Cross.

I released the clutch and the taxi shot forward. At this stage I felt sure that the man I'd knocked down could not have had time to get out of my way. Surely I must have run him over. Was he under my gearbox?

As I pulled away I realised that the intruder in the rear had somehow disappeared but, just as I took this in, another one tried to enter the back as I shot forward. This trapped the new intruder between the door (one of those which opened towards the front of the cab) and the roof. Determined to keep him trapped like that, I slammed the brakes on and off, making the door jerk repeatedly to the front. Whenever I braked I could hear bangs at the rear of the cab. Looking in the mirror, I could see the intruders' army of supporters, who I now realised were chasing me, slam into the back of the taxi.

I continued to accelerate and brake in this fashion to keep my intruder trapped. He then surprised me by falling between the door and the floor so that I was now dragging him along Govan Road, and with the distinct possibility that the beer-can artist was under neath. Pedestrians were screaming at the sight of a taxi dragging a body and followed by an attacking crowd crashing into the rear.

At last I arrived at Govan police station in Orkney Street. I didn't arrive with the passenger I'd tried so hard to keep, and I didn't have the courage to look under the cab in case I found bits of beer-can artist sticking to the gearbox. I ran straight in and confronted the officer with my possible problem.

As he went to inspect my vehicle the first of my comrades arrived to congratulate me on avoiding serious injury, saying he'd seen the whole thing.

Orkney Street Police Station in Govan before its closure.

I expressed surprise that he'd seen it all yet offered no help. His reply shocked me. He said there were two hundred bodies all around me, with battles going on everywhere.

The officer returned to report no body parts under my vehicle. He said my controller had been on the phone to alert him of my predicament and he'd told him a support van was on the scene trying to get me out but it couldn't penetrate the crowd. I felt weak at the knees.

I was soon heading for my control room to pick up a new microphone and continue my shift.

Later I learned that other drivers had operated a shuttle service to the Southern General Hospital Accident and Emergency Department when the commotion died down. More than two dozen bodies were taken to the hospital that evening for repair work.

Needless to say I stopped working the Govan rank for a long time.

GOVAN
ROAD

PAYMENT IN ADVANCE

Getting paid in advance is sometimes, in today's world, a necessity, especially for long journeys at night.

After being paid a £15 fare by a lady customer, I received nothing but hassle all the way to her destination. At the end of the journey she stormed off, slamming the door and hurling abuse at me over the cost of the cab, taking delight in telling me I'd have to go into the rear of the cab to collect payment as she'd thrown it on the floor in disgust.

It's not often I get a £15 tip.

AT THE OTHER END

Reluctantly I agreed to go to Dumbarton at 4am one Friday morning with a male customer who, sounding very convincing, shot me the line that I'd be paid the other end.

After setting off on the £20 journey I felt like kicking myself, I'd had plenty of experience of being duffed at the other end.

Our destination turned out to be a block of flats. My passenger assured me his flatmate knew that money was needed for the fare, he'd only to call on the door-entry intercom to bring him down with the payment.

He left the cab and pressed the entrance button for the flat. Contact was apparently made immediately and the £20 fare was discussed. I was sitting in the cab ten feet away trying to convince myself everything was genuine. Two minutes passed and my passenger made a second call, blasting his flatmate for not appearing with the cash.

'Come on, man,' he called urgently, 'the driver's waiting, he's not got all night. He's looking for his twenty quid. In fact, bring him another two for his patience.'

This cheered me up. A £2 tip would be icing on the cake.

'Sorry driver, but he's on his way, he'll only be a minute. I told him to come straight down when we arrived – sorry!'

I nodded okay.

When I bent down to pick up something from the floor of the cab I heard a squeak I instinctively recognised as the escape route. My £22 had disappeared through the security door.

LOOKS ARE DECEIVING

Every city has its unfortunates, its forgotten few, its outcasts – the wasters, the no-gooders, the homeless, all down on their luck. Usually something dreadful has happened in their lives. Whatever it is, they have not been, perhaps could not have been, allowed back into normal society.

Glasgow Central Station has a taxi rank at the main entrance in Gordon Street which operates twenty-four hours each and every day. During the construction of the railway station a canopy was built as protection from bad weather so that passengers could load or unload their luggage in comfort. The taxi rank runs parallel to the canopy so it shelters people waiting for a cab. A London train arriving at the Central Station may require up to forty cabs to clear the passengers alighting from it. One minute cabs are queuing up looking for work, the next the public are screaming for more to arrive.

It was under this canopy that our unfortunate friends would gather late in the evenings and bed down for the night against the front wall of the station, lying on the iron grids. I used to watch them from my cab on a winter's night, thinking how cold they must be in near freezing temperatures.

I'd be sitting behind the wheel of my cab, my heater on full blast, the engine ticking over to keep the temperature up. Every night they'd gather at the same spot, never moving their sleeping places more than a couple of feet either way.

It wasn't until later that I realised the iron grids were vents for warm air rising from under the station itself. Its constant flow kept them snug as bugs throughout cold nights. Not so daft after all.

On one occasion I brought my two elder sons Stuart and Gordon here to see the homeless sleeping rough, to try to instil in them a sense of concern, to make them realise we should try to give what we can, be it time, aid, comfort or simply respect. We can't tell what they've suffered in earlier times, it may be something horrific – God forbid it should ever happen to us. Some of these people had been through two world wars. A little time and effort spared on them could teach us what they'd suffered.

On a Glasgow housing estate near the Castlemilk shopping centre, one of those built to relieve the pressure on the inner city, there lives an old gentleman who's been hiring cabs for years to take him from his house to the Post Office to collect his pension.

He gets help from Social Services, you can tell this because his jumpers are in the colours of the Glasgow Social Work Department, and come with an identifying badge. He sports a four-day growth of beard all year round. He drools – the results can be seen on his welfare jumper. The worst thing is his body reeks to the point of making you nauseous. You're unable to swallow, it chokes you. It really is that bad. You can understand why local drivers refuse to pick him up.

I make it a point to go to his rescue. By helping him I feel I'm compensating for some of the wrong things I've done in my life. Even if it's just taking him to the Post Office and back, saving his weary legs from standing waiting for a lift.

Earlier this year I went to pick him up from his ground-floor flat, remembering to lower all four windows beforehand. There he was, waiting for me, only this time with a zimmer frame. He got in and the stench was gagging me even before we set off. It was the usual trip to the shops but with a small detour to the library, where he asked me to take the sheet of paper he was holding and have it photocopied. He was going to present the copy to his children and grandchildren so they could remember him after he died.

Not looking at the paper or paying much attention to what he'd

said, I made my way to the library only to find it was closed. Returning to the cab to tell him this, I only then opened the sheet of paper
and could then hardly believe my eyes.

A World War Two Spitfire was spreadeagled across it; Rommel, the
Desert Fox, was pictured in the top right corner; the bottom left
confirmed my passenger's name, Cochrane, RAF Sgt W. Cochrane, a
hero of the Battle of Britain. He'd joined the 8th Army under the
legendary General Montgomery and fought against Field Marshal
Erwin Rommel. Decorated by no less than Winston Churchill himself, he was a Hero of the City of Glasgow Squadron 602 RAF.

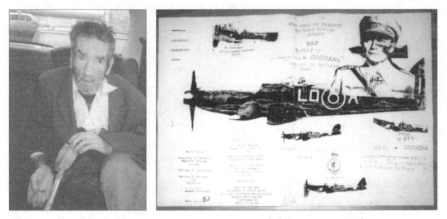

This smelly old man in a
Social Work jumper was
a hero

Rommel, 'The Desert Fox',
with the World War Two Spitfire

I questioned him about the sheet of paper and was astounded by
his history. 'You've done your bit for king and country then,' I said.

'I'm a hero, lad,' he replied. 'Decorated by Winston Churchill. He
called me a hero.'

He pulled up his sleeve to reveal the most beautiful of tattoos on
his inside forearm: a twelve-inch Spitfire exactly as in the picture.
'The Glasgow Squadron 602' and his name and rank were tattooed
underneath. His work of art was still in perfect condition.

'I flew Hurricanes and Spitfires all during the war.'

I tried to imagine him back in 1940, standing on parade in an immaculate uniform, his hair cut to perfection, a Brylcreem Boy. Those days were long gone. Today he was dismissed as a dirty old tramp, but who could hold a candle to this old guy's past?

Try to remember if you can that every old down-and-out has a lot of water flowing under the bridge. Don't be too quick to judge. He might just be a flying ace who saved Britain in times of great need.

RAF Sgt W. Cochrane was indeed one of the few.

NEWSPAPER REPORTERS

In the early 'seventies it was a regular event to pick up a newspaper reporter and photographer and take them to the scene of an accident, robbery or other major incident that would make good copy. Most newspapers now have an account with Glasgow Taxis to pay for such journeys but back then it was done on a daily basis.

One Saturday afternoon I was asked to pick up a reporter and photographer from the *Herald* offices, take them to Airdrie Football Club, then wait and return them after the match was over.

A newspaper workers' home from home – the Press Bar in Albion Street

This was going to be an excellent job for me – a round trip of forty miles and two hours' waiting time.

After I picked them up they requested a stop at the first pub on the way (for a quickie). Both gents got out and after I'd had a thirty-minute wait they came out of the pub and told me they'd decided not to go to Airdrie after all, but I should charge the full price of the job, otherwise the *Herald* would get wind they hadn't attended the game.

They carried on drinking till time was up. When I dropped them back at their offices I asked how they were going to report a match they hadn't seen and they confided to me that they'd phoned a friend who had all the details.

I got paid in full for going nowhere. Thanks, *Glasgow Herald!*

READ ALL ABOUT IT

Daily Hackney

Exclusive Read All About It!

Wednesday 9ᵗʰ April 2003   30p

Ex SNP Leader reduced to Driving cab in Gorbals

Leaving the Gorbals rank one day, I bumped into Alex Salmond and his entourage canvassing for the upcoming local election in April 2003.

My suggestion of a photograph of him behind the wheel of my

cab was greeted with joy. As the unlicensed cabbie took the wheel to pose for the camera, he produced a £5 note to wave out of the window as proof he was only in it for the money (a true politician).

Having allowed the SNP leader to take up 'poll' position, I casually questioned the safety of my cashbox in the cab, within arm's reach of the driver. Someone who was both an unvetted driver and a politician was cause for concern. As you would expect from a politician, he assured me my cash was safe with him (though he'd have his doubts were Tony Blair or Gordon Brown to man the cab).

Naturally that £5 note remained firmly in Alex's possession as he vacated the cab and returned to canvassing.

Thanks Alex – for a millionaire you really are one of the boys.

Did you know that Glasgow Taxis are the cheapest city cabs in Scotland with the exception of Aberdeen?   (July 2003)

A FREE HURL

It was Thursday August 21st 2003 and I'd just completed the last story in this book. I couldn't believe it, after years of writing.

I'd worked through the long list of my memorable experiences, culminating in the story completed on that monumentous day, and felt that a great weight had been lifted from my shoulders. I could now actually look forward to some free time that really was free.

Pulling on to the rank at 9pm that evening, I thought I'd better just flick through my notes and scribbles to make sure everything had actually been written up. It had. The book really had been completed.

Two hours later, again on a rank and at a loose end with nothing to write about, I again scrutinised the notes – just to make sure.

An hour or so later I was stopped at the top of Craigpark in Denniston by a young mother with a 3-year-old. She thanked me for stopping and said if at all possible could I take them to Duke Street, just at the bottom of the hill.

'I know it's a very short distance, driver, but the wean's tired and I know you're going that way anyway. Would you mind very much?'

This wasn't a mother and child hailing a cab to get home in the early hours of the morning, this was a plea for a free hurl. She obviously felt that, as I was going in her direction anyway, payment would be a total waste of her money. Understanding the con but feeling sorry for the child, I agreed to drop them at Duke Street corner.

'Thank you so much driver,' she said, entering the warmth of the cab. 'And wid yi happen to have a wee bag of crisps there fur the wean by any chance?'

'As a matter of fact I do, dear,' was my reply. Amazed at her cheek I continued, 'And what about a wee hot cup of tea for yourself.'

Just when you think it's all over, there's another tale to be told …

What do they say? 'It's not over until the fat lady sings.'

Did you know that to this day automatic cabs in Glasgow number under 5% whereas in London the automatic gearbox is the norm?

THE GREAT EASTERN 'HOTEL'

The Great Eastern 'Hotel' gave a home to many a homeless male over the years, supplying much-needed food and shelter to our less fortunate friends.

The Great Eastern 'Hotel' in Duke Street, formerly Duke Street Cotton Mill, now luxury apartments

Out in the cab one Hogmanay, I stopped at the traffic lights just outside its main entrance, waiting to be on my way to Shettleston with a customer. It was common to see a bunch of patrons of this hostel on the entrance steps, sipping Special Brew and holding court. Unusually for the time of year, there was this evening only one lone figure sitting dejectedly on the steps.

I turned away from observing the old boy and caught sight of the carry-out I'd fetched earlier from the off licence. If I could offer him a drink, I thought, maybe it would cheer him up a bit. Picking up two cans of beer, I dangled them out of the window to attract his attention. No joy.

I gave two small blasts of the horn. Still no joy.

He must have seen me. Perhaps he was afraid to come up and take the bait in case I drove off with the beer still in my hand, laughing at him. There was no movement in the stubborn old guy.

The traffic lights changed. It was time for me to roll. I swung my arm out and flicked my wrist in a throwing motion. The two cans became airborne, flying towards the steps just in front of him and landing on the street with a thud.

This had its effect on my cautious observer. Nobody could recognise the sound of two full beer cans hitting the ground better than he could. It fired him with enthusiasm. His despondency was transformed into an urgent rush to retrieve the beer from the the roadside before anyone beat him to it or a passing vehicle squashed the cans.

I could see him in my rear-view mirror. The steps and the cans were only about ten feet apart but unfortunately for the old boy there was an obstacle in the form of a safety barrier running right across the entrance, making a direct approach impossible. Jumping over the fence was out of the question by forty years – to retrieve the bounty he was going to have to circumnavigate it. He realised that a run was required but running had eluded him for about as long as his jumping career.

It was what happened next that gave me most pleasure.

He spurted into a sort of ballet dancer's trot, trying to run on tiptoes to corner the far end of the barrier as quick as he could. It made me cry with laughter. What a sight to behold – it really filled me with emotion.

'HAPPY NEW YEAR, OLD BUDDIE!' I found myself shouting.

Later I felt so sorry that at his time of life so much depended on two cans of beer, but at least I'd been able to give a little joy.

I worked out on paper later that I've probably drunk six cans of beer a week since I was 18. That's a staggering TEN THOUSAND cans – but I can really only remember two.

NORTH HANOVER QUICKIE

The North Hanover Street rank in the City Centre, at the corner of George Square, just outside Queen Street Station, operates from midnight to 6am.

About 4am one bright morning, as the taxis started to rank up, drivers congregated round the first cab on the rank, standing about talking, having a laugh. At the same time we observed two middle-aged tramps chatting each other up on a park bench on empty ground left by the demolition of a once-proud building. They were steadily consuming the remains of a bottle of Lanlique, the cheap but potent brew commonly known as 'Lani'. Relations between the pair were becoming extremely amorous as the Lani took effect.

We watched with glee as the loving pair moved from the bench to the comfort of the grass, jeering and clapping as they assumed a mating position. Quite unperturbed by their audience, their bonking carried on till it earned them a standing ovation from admirers.

Then they returned to their bench and carried on their conversation as if nothing had happened.

OFF THE BEATEN TRACK

Leaving the house one morning about 8am I got a call for a pick-up in Cathkin Braes Road near Cathkin, deep in the South Side, just outside the city border. I had some trouble finding the place.

After driving up and down the lonely road several times, I spotted a golfer with clubs and trolley heading for the golf club. He lived locally but didn't recognise the address. He suggested I try the clubhouse as there were private houses in the grounds, but this brought no success. Contacting my radio room for clarification didn't bring immediate results either. I parked and awaited further instructions while they tried to get on to the Education authorities who'd ordered the cab and had an account with our company.

The pick-up was now twenty minutes late. There were no buildings along this desolate stretch of road and no person to be seen. Not wanting to appear stupid for failing to find the address, I cruised fruitlessly once again, without success.

What I did find, however, was a gap in the hedgerow with tracks leading to the golf course. On the golf course was a tractor, with two greenkeepers hard at work.

Well, instead of just waiting on the radio room I might as well ask the greenkeepers' advice. They too were stumped but they said there was a row of cottages further down the track, just over the hill. I went further into the golf course, approximately another three fairways, and having come this far thought a little further wouldn't kill me.

Over the hill, I drove into a car park surrounded by terraces of farm cottages. White steam belching from the exhaust of a Mercedes 4x4 was a giveaway that there was life somewhere. I got out of the cab and tried to find a house number or name but could see none.

The driver's door of the Mercedes flew open. The infuriated mother of the schoolchild in the car launched straight into the offensive – no 'Good morning driver,' or 'I see you managed to find the address.' No, straight for the jugular, screeching like a wife when you stott in from the pub feeling pleased with yourself only to find out your guests for the evening just gave up and went home in disgust.

'This is an absolute disgrace! This car was booked by the City Council for 8.30am. You're thirty minutes late! Thanks to the incompetence of you and your company, not only is my child late for school, but I am late for a very important meeting – which I've probably missed by now.'

The rat-tat-tat of the well-trained machine-gun tongue never missed a beat or paused to draw breath. She seemed well versed in the art of attack. I decided to look stupid until she'd burned herself out or decided time was precious.

Undoubtedly this was my hire. I just had to wait patiently for the mouth of the Clyde Tunnel to shut so that I could ask her name and confirm I had the right address. The dreaded sigh from the irate parent came when I was able to ask the question. You could see her thinking, *Why am I surrounded by complete idiots?*

It was obvious to me that the address I'd been given was not the pick-up address. This was more than a quarter of a mile from the road and you had to cross four fairways to get to it. Saying that the entrance from the main road was obscure was an understatement. 'Hole in the wall' more like – no signpost, no clue there were houses down the track. What chance did a taxi driver have of finding it?

I confronted the lady who by this time had cooled down just enough to let me speak. I'm an experienced driver, my job is to find addresses, but in all my years of driving a cab I've never come across a worse described address. It's taken me half an hour to find your house while my company's been doing its best to help me; the Education Department's also been informed and no doubt they too are trying to find out where you live – and all so that your child can be taken to school.

I suggested that if she instead of the local authority had to pick up the bill for the taxi then perhaps the outcome would have been different.

'What do you mean by that?' she snapped.

'For a start you'd probably take your own child a mile and a half to school in your own Mercedes. But let's say you didn't have a car … surely you'd have phoned my office to ask where the cab was and been able to give directions.'

I might have been talking to a brick wall. She went over to her car and switched the engine off.

'You do know, driver, that I'm escorting my child to school and that you're bringing me back here?'

Typical. The Council was in fact going to have to pay double.

I watched mother and daughter enter the cab. Although recovering from a broken leg, there was absolutely no need for this child to be escorted – she was perfectly capable of entering and leaving the taxi by herself.

I drove mother and child to school and returned the mother. Nothing at all was said during the journey and a short but truculent acknowledgement was made at its end.

This was not quite the end of the story. The scorned mother's final attack was a letter of complaint to the taxi office about my behaviour and remarks. None of it was her fault.

Something is wrong in society when everyone blames everyone else. Too many people just take whatever they can get for nothing, never mind that *somebody* has to pay.

THE RUCHILL OFF LICENCE

In the late 'nineties the Glasgow cab trade experienced a number of robberies from cabs.

In some areas youths would simply try to steal the cash box. The smallest boy would provoke the driver into getting out of his cab to chase him away, then a talented companion would make a swift entry for the prize. These kids are very streetwise and live by their wits. It was in the Possilpark/Ruchill area that most of the robberies were taking place.

It was no surprise to me when I heard of one driver being robbed. He was strong and robust, quite capable of handling himself and, according to what I heard, eager to get involved and show our little friends that tackling him would be the mistake of their lives.

We were warned several times over the air one evening to be vigilant in these areas as the gangs of youths were out in force. This driver worked the area and knew what to expect.

During his shift he spotted a group of youths outside the off licence in Bilsland Drive, Ruchill, just down the road from Possilpark, so decided to replenish his stock of lager. He went into the off licence, knowing full well he'd left his cash box in full view. The cab windows were down, the doors unlocked.

He waited patiently inside the shop, a routine customer. Secretly he was desperate to pounce on anyone who took the bait. He could see the local talent mingling outside as he stood in the queue. In turn each surveyed the cab, unable to decide if it was too good to be true.

Watching with bated breath from inside the shop window our driver heard a sudden *Rat-at-at-at-at-at-at-at-at-at-at-at-at*-BANG.

Not a machine gun, something far, far worse – the sound of the shop's roller shutters closing, trapping customers inside.

You have to admire the boys' devious minds. Blood vessels burst in our frustrated driver's face. He watched helplessly as his money was divided up and the taxi was ransacked. There was no rush to carve up the spoils – the customers were not released until well after the local talent had gone to ground.

ROYSTON ROAD ROBBERS

One evening when I was travelling along Royston Road I was frantically flagged down by a man of about thirty carrying two suitcases and at least two holdalls.

With the wall behind him, there seemed no escape from the robbers on Royston Road

'Thank God you've stopped, driver! I'm trying to get away from that gang of youths,' he gasped.

I looked over to where he was pointing and, sure enough, several members of the local talent were waiting to pounce.

'Thank God I'm safe! If you hadn't come along when you did that lot would've robbed me for sure.'

He directed me to take him to a nearby block of high-rise flats. When we got there he told me he had no money for the £1.50 fare.

'But you can have some of these CDs, driver – all brand new.'

Feeling sorry for him, I declined the generous offer. 'As long as you're safe mate,' I said, 'that's the main thing.'

I reassured him that some decent people out here still care for each other.

'Aw, driver,' came his reply, 'Ah could niver huv shown face in this neighbourhood again if they'd robbed me of awe this gear. Specially since Ah've jist broke into that wee shope doon there ti git it.'

Did you know that it's not the very small journeys that annoy taxi drivers, it's the time in between them?

ROUND THE BEND

Some passengers like to repeat themselves to make quite sure you know exactly what they mean, just in case you turn left instead of right and cost them an extra 20p. This is a not uncommon list of instructions:

'Driver, as you go round this bend its the third on the left … Yeah, just third on the left, driver … That's right, not the first on the left … not the second on the left … the third on the left. This one here, driver … That's right, this one here.'

Is it me? Do I look like a complete idiot?

Did you know that many customers insist on giving the driver directions in the form of hand signals? When he's sitting directly in front of them facing the same way! A pair of eyes in the back of the head would be a distinct advantage.

CALLIPER JANE

Like every city Glasgow has its ladies of the night. For years the red-light district has been known as Blythswood Square. They've long since moved about four hundred yards away but their beat is still called Blythswood Square.

They also congregate at the Charing Cross coffee stall which stays open well into the night.

I used to pick up one of the ladies from various parts of the city and drop her off at the stall to await business. Over time I got talking to her. It was mostly regular customers that she had, regular bookings for, say, every Wednesday at 10pm, picking her up at the coffee stall. She'd make her own way back by taxi.

Her name was Jane. She was a nice person – no obvious similarities to a cliché prostitute. She wore a calliper on one leg. I hadn't thought of a prostitute wearing a calliper before. During one of our

The Charing Cross fountain (toilet) and coffee stall

conversations she politely told me that her customers didn't even mention her disability, it was no big deal, she didn't wear the calliper in bed.

And sometimes you'd see Jane wearing a second calliper.

One fine summer's day she flagged me down outside her close in Shettleston Road in the East End. She had her husband and two children with her – they were off for a day out at the fine park at Hogganfield Loch.

I was very discreet, kidding I didn't recognise her.

She sent me reeling when, at the end of the journey, she asked me to pick them up for the trip home, then carry on to the coffee stall as one of her regulars would be picking her up at 6pm.

I thought at first she'd put her foot in it, but the husband heard everything and didn't bat an eyelid.

After we'd dropped the family off I told her I'd picked up three American sailors the night before, around 3am, who'd said they'd been looking for a woman and could I recommend anywhere that was still open. I was sorry to disappoint them but by 3am everything's finished.

I should have brought them up to her house, Jane replied, 3am's okay – business is business.

'What about your husband?'

Clear as a bell she replied, 'He just goes to bed next door till I'm finished, no problem.'

SLEEPING BEAUTY TO STIRLING

My son Gordon was asked one Friday night to take a young lady to Stirling. It was around 2am. As usual for that time of night, he requested payment in advance. The fare was £40. She was happy to pay, so the hire commenced.

Not long into the journey Gordon noticed the passenger was fast asleep. Having been given Stirling town centre as the destination, he let her sleep on until they were approaching the railway station. Awakened, she asked where she'd been taken and, receiving the reply, said it wasn't where she wanted to be. She was reminded she'd paid the fare before leaving Glasgow, but insisted on being taken back to the pick-up point.

He drove her back to George Square, where she thanked him very much and left the cab.

MATCH DAY

Any book about Glasgow needs a football story or two.

Let me start by assuring you that my upbringing was in no way religiously prejudiced. My father Archie was a Partick Thistle supporter and at Firhill Park I saw them get many a good thrashing from almost every other club.

Now it's well known how deeply Glasgow is divided into two main football factions, Rangers and Celtic, or Celtic and Rangers as others would prefer. This story could go on for ever if I tried to go into their history and religious background. I'm content to scratch the surface.

Parkhead, home of Celtic Football Club

For years I've driven cabs to both Parkhead and Ibrox Park and enjoyed or suffered the banter from both sides. Supporters heading for these matches are all excitedly anticipating victory and most are in good humour. It's rare to have trouble before kick-off – afterwards is of course a different story. Tribal camaraderie generated between supporters during the match, the 'affluence of incohol' and defeat or victory can turn happy supporters nasty and violent. I've seen many confrontations between supporters, all ugly and full of evil. It can be very frightening. Serious injury and even death can result.

There's nothing more terrifying for a cabbie than to be caught between two angry groups of opposing supporters and with nowhere to go, trapped perhaps in a line of traffic.

Rangers Football Club's Ibrox stadium

It's worst when it's the Glasgow Old Firm (the big two) and the religious chants can barely be heard above the crash of missiles and the odd Buckfast bottle whistling past you, looking for a spare body to knock some sense into. Facing up to either faction would be suicide. The bitterness between them, the anger shown on these occasions, is unimaginable.

This brings me to my next point – which may well contradict what I've just said.

Partick Thistle Football Club at Firhill

There is one, only one, occasion that brings the old adversaries together: when Scotland, our glorious national football team, is ready to wage war on the field against another country ... say — just to pick one at random — England, 'the auld enemy'.

Our supporters are then totally united under one banner, the Saltire, the St Andrews Cross ... or is it two banners with the Lion Rampant?

It was in the late 'seventies that I heard about football casuals from England organising themselves for a little excursion to our national stadium, Hampden Park. They were obviously in search of a little extra excitement after the final whistle, something that I'm told English games lack from time to time.

I was working that day and witnessed a confrontation at Polmadie Road and Calder Street, about a mile from the park. It didn't last very long, wise English supporters soon reading the writing on the wall (something like: 'We've bitten off more than we can chew, lads,' or 'Let's get to f**k out of here!') The Tartan Army flew after them, kilts and tartan scarves swinging as muscle-bound legs thundered down Polmadie Road.

I believe there was mayhem at Central Station and several running battles took place between the stadium and City Centre.

A signpost points the way to Hampden

To be honest, I don't think the English supporters had ever encountered such an arrogant and united bunch of men. After the match the English retreat was mainly on foot — it's impossible for taxis and buses to cope with the demands of more than fifty thousand bodies spewing onto the street at one time. Everyone was trying to make transport connections or be first back to his local for the postmortem.

Provocation was the name of the game that day, not football.

Widely respected throughout the world, the famous Tartan Army has been welcomed wherever it has gone. I don't think any country can boast a more fun-loving and true following than the Scots.

Every true Scottish supporter wants to uphold the reputation of our travelling army – even Glasgow cabbies.

Throughout the day of an international match, taxi drivers are busy shuttling supporters from airports, stations and various pubs throughout the city. Many will have travelled up from cities down south, many have come to make a weekend of it. The football spirit hits them all. You see droves of supporters converging on the stadium in various modes of transport. I always feel sorry for the coach drivers, with all the bellowing and stamping of feet they have to endure as their motley crews rehearse for the main arena. Taxis suffer the banging and stamping too, only not on so large a scale.

Hampden Park, Scotland's National Stadium

You can see why many older drivers don't work the football matches. They feel they've done their fair share in their heyday and by now have earned the right to pack up early and wait for a less stressful time to work. That's only right. Leave the hassle to the fresh blood in the trade – the previous generation did the same to them.

Next time the Auld Enemy comes to Hampden Park you may just find me with an armchair ticket to watch the match, not worrying about getting a cab home.

A GLIMPSE OF THE JOCK STEIN LEGEND

Around 1am one summer's night I picked up a middle-aged gentleman who told me to take him to Southwood Drive in King's Park and wait for him while he went into a house. He'd only be a short while, then I was to drive him to his own house.

He was getting no reply at the house in Southwood Drive, but after much banging on the door and shouts of 'Jock' an upstairs window at last opened and a growling male responded. It didn't sound as if he had any intention of being polite to my customer.

At this point I sat up and started to take notice.

Normally you could hear a pin drop in this sleepy little road. Not tonight.

I'd heard enough by this time to realise that 'Jock' was Jock Stein as in 'Celtic Football Manager', a man with many words for suggesting someone should be somewhere else.

Jock Stein led the team that defeated the famous Internazionale Milan 2-1 in the final of the European Champions Cup in 1967

Our Jock was giving it pelters! His beauty sleep had been disturbed by an undesirable and the football legend was not short of a few choice words.

Unknown to me, Jock had just moved into this house and my fare was the previous owner who, after a barrelful, had decided to pay his new mate a visit to see how he was settling in. He got a rather different response to the one he was expecting.

I drove a very disappointed Mr Friendly back to his own house.

Did you know that On June 16th 2004 Hoopy the Celtic mascot and the legend Danny McGrain waved off the 58th Annual Taxi outing to Ayrshire for eight hundred underprivileged and special needs kids? Celtic's Charity Fund has been the main sponsor of the event for the last five years, this year donating several thousand pounds for the outing to Troon. Taxi drivers and their helpers happily give their time and join a convoy of two hundred and fifty cabs heading for a day of fun, with a disco, games and street party.

Hoopy
followed by
a pipe band
before
leaving for
the outing
to Troon.

HASTE YE BACK!

Most Glasgow taxi drivers will tell you that the first thing tourists comment on is how friendly Glasgow people are. They're always willing to stop what they're doing and give a few moments of their time. This doesn't happen in most other cities.

The second thing they'll say is how beautiful the city is, expressing surprise at our wonderful architecture.

When I'm driving tourists around my priority is to make them feel comfortable and welcome. Then I always ask the same question: 'How long will you be staying in Glasgow?'

It breaks my heart that the answer is usually something like: 'We're only here today and tomorrow. We didn't realise how lovely your city is and how friendly the people are, or we'd have arranged to stay longer.'

But they'll often add: 'We've enjoyed Glasgow so much we're planning to return next year – we've had such a wonderful time!'

GLASGOW AIRPORT

Glasgow Airport has its own licensed taxi fleet to shuttle customers to the City Centre. No longer are the Black Hacks able to rank there to take our customers from our airport to our city.

The Glasgow taxi meeting point outside the main terminal building

When they first licensed their own fleet and expelled our vehicles from the rank it was a huge blow to the taxi trade. About a hundred cabs that had worked the airport rank were now forced to ply for hire in the city. This made things even more difficult for the trade, already suffering as the population of Glasgow was falling steadily year on year. Absorbing another hundred cabs took its toll and there was a knock-on effect to the general public and business community. If you want a taxi to the airport now you pay over the odds – the airport taxis are the most expensive in the Glasgow area.

The only way Glasgow cabs can get a return journey from the airport to the city now is if the customer phones 429 7070. We offer a substantial discount for airport-bound passengers who want a return journey without paying 'the Big Price'. Many of our customers take up the offer not just on grounds of cost but for convenience – an airport car can't compete with a Black Hack when it comes to luggage space, and often an annual holiday requires that extra wee bit of baggage.

It's only rarely that a customer has to wait more than five minutes for a Glasgow Taxis cab to meet them at the pick-up point outside the main terminal.

So – support your Black Hack cabbie and save yourself a few bob. And tell him you heard about it here!

... VIA THE OLD TOLL BAR

A hire from the South Side to Glasgow Airport was quoted a price of £15. It was a radio job and I got the call to pick up the two businessmen.

As soon as they enter the cab I usually ask airport-bound passengers when they have to check in, then I give them a road report and estimated time of arrival. This usually goes down well as many don't have a clue how long it takes to get to the airport, especially if they're visitors.

Drivers are kept informed of any hold-ups, and given alternative routes to keep delays to a minimum. When no traffic report is broadcast it's safe to assume there's no delay. A typical journey from City Centre to airport will take fifteen or twenty minutes.

When I picked up my passengers I followed this routine. They told me they had an hour before check-in. Could I recommend a nice pub to stop at on the way? They didn't want a hotel, they'd been living in hotels for the past week.

The Old Toll Bar in the heart of the docklands, near Govan Road, immediately sprang to mind. It wouldn't take us off the route to the airport, and it was one of my favourite pubs. Remember the old pubs your grandfather used to talk about – with wooden floors and old McEwan's Pale Ale mirrors on the walls? The mirrors here were ten feet long and four feet wide, with beautifully engraved

The gantry at the Old Toll Bar

advertising slogans and the price of a pint, 1/6d.

The gantry is decorated with old beer barrels, carved, highly varnished — and absolutely beautiful!

I suggested to my two businessmen that The Old Toll Bar was the place for a quiet pint in good surroundings. I dropped them at the pub and they promised to return in five minutes.

After twenty minutes they came out and told me they'd be having another drink. They were enjoying the pub so much, and the 'Glasga patter', that they'd rescheduled their departure and were staying another day.

I reflected ruefully that my £15 fare to the airport was up the Swanee. It looked like all I'd be getting was the £5 showing on the meter.

They said they'd be staying at the pub. They collected their luggage and thanked me profusely for my choice of drinking establishment. And they paid me the original fare quoted — £15! Everyone was a winner and Glasgow had two happy visitors for another night.

BUCK-A-LOO STREET

Depending on where people come from and their accents, it can be very hard to understand what they're saying.

The Chinese are most difficult of all, their pronunciation of a street name can be totally different. Those born and brought up in this country are fine, but members of the older generation often can't speak a word of English. They sometimes get round the problem by producing a card or note with the address printed on it.

One elderly Chinese gentleman leaving the casino at 4am entered my cab and asked for 'Buck-a-loo Street'.

Not remotely recognising it from his pronunciation, I asked him to repeat the address.

'Buck-a-loo Street,' came the reply once more.

And a third time. This time the tone of his voice had changed to one of irritation. Sitting in a taxi going nowhere because the driver was too stupid to understand him turned his irration into frustration. He began to shout at me:

'Buck-a-loo Street!

'*Buck-a-loo Street!*

'Buck-a-loo Street!'

He was trying to tell me what an idiot I was.

Racking my brains to save my Chinese friend from a heart attack, it eventually dawned on me that he must mean Buccleuch Street, in Garnethill. Arriving at this destination, I tried to explain to him the nuances of correct pronunciation. He nodded sagely in agreement and confirmed the address for the final time with great relief:

'Oh yes! Buck-a-loo Street.'

Makes me wonder what his version of 'As Hoe!' would be.

BLACK LADY TO CENTRAL STATION

It was December 1973 and, as I turned into St Vincent Street from Argyle Street, a black woman holding a baby wrapped in a shawl hailed my cab.

Please would I take her to Central Station, and could I bring her luggage from inside the close as she was pregnant and couldn't carry heavy cases herself. I agreed and went to pick up what I thought would be a case or two. On entering the close I counted eight suitcases awaiting me.

It was a time when racial discrimination was making headlines. I could just see the story in one of the tabloids: 'Glasgow Taxi Driver Leaves Pregnant Black Lady in Despair as she Misses Train to Congo'.

I picked up the first two cases and loaded them into the cab, returning for more. A quick recount of the remaining luggage confirmed that there were eight suitcases still waiting. I thought I must have counted wrongly first time. When I counted eight again on the second return trip I realised that another person in a flat was replenishing the stock.

I drew the situation of the multiplying suitcases to the attention of the black lady. She confirmed that was the last of the luggage to go. Several journeys later I had about twenty suitcases in my cab and no room for mother and child.

By this time I'd been in the flat to check out this moonlight removal and sussed out I'd need another cab. I radioed for back-up from my vehicle and duly carried out the remainder of the luggage to the pavement to pre-empt the next driver's complaints about being a taxi and not Pickford's.

The second cab duly arrived, driven by what looked like the oldest driver in the trade. He complained of a bad back which prevented him from lifting anything heavier than a 2lb bag of sugar.

Smiling nevertheless and giving my fellow driver a warm welcome, I assured him I'd do all the loading and unloading myself – I was fit as a fiddle and anxious to offer the best of unbiased Glasgow hospitality.

Wiping the sweat from my brow, I packed as much as possible of what remained of the flitting into the second cab, leaving only the carpets, pots and pans which would require a third cab. Eventually we set off.

Arriving at the Central Station I luckily spotted a porter. Porters in those days would transport passengers' luggage on huge barrows – this barrow had an iron framework and was capable of carrying forty suitcases. The nice man saw our problem and, when I described the wonderful gratuity he'd soon be rewarded with, helped transfer the contents of the two cabs to his barrow.

An hour and a half after stopping for the black lady my cab was finally empty; the second taxi was also empty; the porter was totally exhausted. All that remained was to take the fare. Clearly the standard 10/- was out of the question – by now I was looking to be paid for two hours' work, plus an hour for the other cabbie.

When told a payment of £5 was expected for the house removal, the lady flew into a tantrum and screamed she was being robbed. This performance drew a large sympathetic crowd. Onlookers could see at a glance how two street cabbies were ripping off this discriminated-against pregnant woman bravely clutching her child.

The tantrum lasted several minutes. Eventually, opening her purse, she declared she had no money for the taxis. All she had was a £5 note and this was not for us, it was for getting her to Heathrow.

To prove her point she pulled out the fiver and turned her purse upside down. I immediately snatched the note for the cab fares and felt totally justified in doing so.

A look of shock and horror broke out on her face. Screaming for the police, she ran down the platform and disappeared.

Laughing, the other driver and I paid the porter and split the rest of the £5 between us. It was a well-deserved, hard-earned fare.

As we were about to leave, the porter shouted after us. What was to happen to the barrowful of luggage?

'I don't know, you're the porter, not me.'

He replied in true Glaswegan tones, 'Porter f**k all – I'm here to deliver the newspapers!'

NOT ANY OLD SUNDAY MORNING

At 5am one Sunday morning in June 1971 my night-shift driver changed over with me and I ran him home before starting work.

It was usually very quiet on a Sunday morning, so I'd set my earnings target very low. I wanted £5 by noon, that being my finishing time, for a drivers' reunion in the local pub.

Almost immediately I received a call to pick up at Calderwood, East Kilbride and take a lady customer to Glasgow Airport. I instantly perked up. The fare to Glasgow Airport from her address was £6.

The entrance to Glasgow Airport

That job would give me £5 clear of fuel. Anything else would be a bonus.

Arriving at the address, I received a wave from her first-floor flat window to let me know she was on her way down. She appeared carrying a box and two suitcases.

'The suitcases,' she said, 'are going with me to Italy. This box is for you, driver.'

It was loaded with goodies that would not keep fresh for the time she'd be on holiday:

> 1 loaf of bread
> 2 pints of milk
> ½lb of cheese
> 6 eggs
> ½lb of bacon
> 3 slices of black pudding.

A fabulous start to the day!

On reaching the airport, I thanked her very much for the goodies and the £6 fare.

I was soon on my way back, having earned my expected morning's total though it was still only 6am. Entering East Kilbride, travelling along the dual carriageway, I was frantically flagged down by a motorist on the other side of the road.

I about-turned at the roundabout ahead and drew up beside him.

'Driver, thank God! I'm desperate to get to Prestwick Airport! My car's broken down...'

I couldn't believe my luck!

The fare to Prestwick was £15 but he said if I got him there in an hour he'd pay £20!

We set off at once, travelling over the Eaglesham Moors – so often an extremely foggy place, as it was this day. At the top of the moor sheep were mingling in the middle of the road as I tried to negotiate a passage through them.

At Prestwick I was paid the promised £20 by a truly delighted customer who'd thought his world was coming to an end – there's no way he could have made it there in time without me.

On the return journey I began thinking about those sheep mingling on the misty moor. What would I do if I was presented with a freshly killed sheep lying there in front of me?

Before very long I was confronted with exactly that scenario. In the deep fog, just having been struck a fatal blow by an articulated lorry travelling in the opposite direction, the carcass of a sheep lay in my path.

Was my luck in today? Should I take this as a good omen?

Without too much thought, just a tremor of guilt, I stopped the old FX4, opened the luggage compartment, removed the mat and hastily heaved in the warm carcass. Covering the spoils with the mat, I took off again within seconds.

There seemed to me to be nothing wrong with this – the next vehicle would surely have run it over. But what was I going to do with this bloody sheep?

George McDonald's was the name that sprang to mind. He was a taxi driver with a knowledge of fishing and hunting. You could go into George's kitchen for a cup of tea and find the sink full of trout waiting to be gutted, or rabbits lying on the worktops. I drove to George's and told him the tale.

'You're in luck, Jack. My old friend Sandy'll be here in half an hour. You remember Sandy, don't you? The shepherd from the Isle of Sanda?'

My strange luck continued. On seeing the sheep Sandy felt immediately at home. Checking out George's garage, he decided to skin
it in there. With a sharp kitchen knife he slit the hind legs just above
the ankles, inserted the extension bar from a socket set through the
openings and strung the sheep up with a block and tackle.

'Leave it there for a week, lads. The blood'll have drained by that
time. It'll be ready to cook.'

It was now 11am. I was due in the pub at noon and decided to
finish work an hour early.

My morning's earnings were:

> £26 in cash
> 1 loaf of bread
> 2 pints of milk
> ½ lb of cheese
> 6 eggs
> ½ lb of bacon
> 3 slices of black pudding.
> 1 sheep.

Not bad for a Sunday morning.

'DYING' AT THE GLASGOW MUSIC-HALLS

I chauffeured Bob Monkhouse about Glasgow for
a week when he was holding auditions at the Plaza Ballroom for a
TV show. He told me about the days when he was young, when
comedians had to run the gauntlet of Glasgow audiences.

If a comedian was liked then he didn't have rotten fruit and veg
thrown at him. It was well known in the entertainment industry
that, if you got past a Glaswegian audience, you were on the road
to success.

The Glasgow people, while having a most wonderful heart, do
not suffer fools gladly.

It's the same today – ask any Glasgow cabbie who takes a wrong
turn!

RICKI'S EMPTY CHAIR

Returning from holiday early in February 2004, I learned of the death of one of Glasgow's best-loved comedians, Ricki Fulton. For years he'd brought joyful laughter to millions.

I remembered him from my visits to Glasgow theatres as a young lad. He did a stand-up routine with Jack Milroy, they were the famous duo Francie and Jossie. Ricki became a vital part of the Scottish New Year, appearing on TV hogmanay shows as the Rev I.M. Jolly and lecturing the nation on his misfortunes.

Sadly Ricki had been diagnosed with Alzheimers. A terminal illness is a heartbreaking experience for both patient and family: enormnous demands are put upon everyone affected.

When I returned to work next day every cabbie was talking about Ricki, the older drivers about all the years he and his family had been hiring our cabs, and how long it had been since they had picked him up.

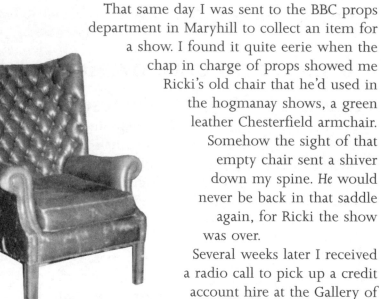

That same day I was sent to the BBC props department in Maryhill to collect an item for a show. I found it quite eerie when the chap in charge of props showed me Ricki's old chair that he'd used in the hogmanay shows, a green leather Chesterfield armchair. Somehow the sight of that empty chair sent a shiver down my spine. He would never be back in that saddle again, for Ricki the show was over.

Several weeks later I received a radio call to pick up a credit account hire at the Gallery of Modern Art in Queen Street and take the customer to the West End. The name of the credit-account holder was Ricki Fulton!

I arrived and the pick-up point and was really delighted to see Ricki's wife Kate approaching the cab with her friend. Kate looked absolutely beautiful in her summer dress, a walking-stick in her hand for support. I could only think of the rough time she'd had supporting her husband through the darkness of his illness, then the strain of the funeral. My heart went out to her as I drove her home on that fine sunny day. I couldn't find the courage to say anything to her, I just let the two of them talk to each other.

When she left the cab she gave me a £2 tip and thanked me for the pleasant drive home. To tell you the truth, I didn't want any money from her but I didn't wish to appear ungrateful. I managed to wish her a better year next year. I felt like saying I'd have considered it an honour to drive her home for nothing.

All the very best, Kate.

THE MURDER OF JOHN WALKINSHAW

I knew him as Uncle John. He was a close friend of our family, in particular my father Archie and his brother Peter. Together with Bernard Finningham, Peter's brother-in-law, they made quite a foursome. All were Glasgow taxi drivers. They shared the highs and lows of the trade.

John Walkinshaw stayed in Horndean Crescent, Queenslie, near Easterhouse with his wife Helen and three daughters, Betty aged 16, Frances 9, Helen 7. He was a kind man. Slim build. Anti-violent.

John Walkinshaw
in his FX3 cab

About 1.45am on Sunday morning July 23rd 1961 he dropped a hire in Tormusk Road in Castlemilk. It was to be the last hire John Walkinshaw would ever carry out.

Two shots from a handgun startled the residents of Tormusk Road. They came out to investigate. The engine of UVM 766 was still running. John was slumped over the wheel, two point-blank shots in his head, fired through the windscreen. There was blood everywhere. John lay dying.

Emergency calls came into the radio room and the police, ambulance and fellow taxi drivers were urgently dispatched to the scene. Soon the quiet little road in Castlemilk was crammed with taxis and

BAILEY HOUSE

TORMUSK ROAD

police cars. John was taken by ambulance to the Victoria Infirmary and later transferred to Killearn Hospital.

Being a very close friend, my father was taken by the police to sit at John's bedside and talk to him, encouraging him to regain consciousness. He never did.

John Walkinshaw died of gunshot wounds to the head at the age of 36. There was no motive for the killing, which caused untold grief and suffering. It was a pointless waste of a good life.

At his funeral in Riddrie a uniformed piper from the Cameronians, John's old regiment, led the half-mile-long cortege.

R.I.P. Victor 25.

Walter Scott Ellis

Walter Scott Ellis was the man charged with his murder. He appeared at the High Court in Glasgow; the trial lasted four days. There was no witness to the shooting and the murder weapon was never found. Circumstantial evidence and the fact that Ellis was shown to have lied about his whereabouts at the time of the murder worked for the prosecution. Bullets were found in a flat where Ellis had been staying, and, though they were not the same as the bullets that killed John, it was established that they could have been fired from the gun used that night.

In summing up, the judge Lord Patrick told the jury: 'The proof in this case, if there was proof, would depend wholly on circumstantial evidence. People sneer at that but these are uninformed people who do not understand that it is every bit as reliable as other evidence. Very often there are no eyewitnesses to a crime, and everything depends on circumstantial evidence.'

He stressed the seriousness of the crime: 'If the accused is found guilty he will be hanged by the neck. But that is not a concern of yours or mine.' Some members of the jury winced slightly at this. 'You are here to hear the evidence and make up your minds on that.'

The jury retired. It was thought that, following a complicated four-day trial, they would be out for some time but, to everyone's surprise, the jury bell rang after only half an hour. Ellis rose and in a silent courtroom the foreman of the jury gave their verdict, 'Not proven – unanimously.'

Ellis was pictured on the front page of one newspaper smoking a cigar and jubilantly celebrating. He had sold his story for £100 and was quoted as saying, 'I think John Walkinshaw was shot by a raving madman lurking in the Castlemilk woods – by a man who may strike again. I had nothing at all to do with this ghastly, pointless murder.'

It was the high point of Ellis's criminal career. Always keen on armed robbery and boastful that he had cheated the gallows and could flaut the law, he became too casually confident and was cornered trying to hold up a bank in Pollokshaws in 1966. Sentencing him to a punitive twenty-one years for attempted murder and armed robbery, the judge said that while he was at large the lives of innocent members of the public were at risk.

Ellis served only fourteen years, but a few months after his release in 1980 he made a bungled attempt at holding up a licensed grocery shop with a replica gun. He was sentenced to another three years.

After John's death his taxi call sign, 'Victor 25', was never used again.

THE DAY OF THE IBROX DISASTER

It started off like any other day. The morning was quiet. Towards lunchtime began the usual slow build-up of supporters making their way to pubs to meet up with companions.

It was January 2nd 1971, the day of the Glasgow Derby: the Auld Firm would clash at Ibrox Stadium; a capacity crowd of 80,000 was expected, divided into two halves. Green and white hoops would adorn the Celtic end, a sea of blue and white the Rangers home end.

I was about 19 years old at this time and working in East Kilbride. I'd be driving my cab before, during and after the match. I knew every taxi driver would see *something* happen on a day like this, but I and others were totally unprepared for the carnage of that fateful afternoon.

The memorial at
Ibrox Stadium

The build-up for the match continued. Singing and chanting was heard from the thriving public bars as supporters began pouring onto the streets to make their way to the ground for the 3 o'clock kick-off. Trains, trams, coaches, minibuses, cars and taxis were all bursting at the seams. Road-users jostled for position in traffic jams just to be there that all-important few seconds earlier.

Soon it was 3 o'clock and the game burst into life.

It's around this time that taxis are very quiet, having coped with the mad rush to the match and last-minute desperados who'd spent too long nattering in the pub. It would be 90 minutes before the exodus.

Not being a football fan, I wasn't listening to the game on the radio, I was paying more attention to the weather which was getting increasingly foggy. Soon thousands of supporters would be spilling out of the stadium – many would leave that minute or two before the game ended to be ahead of the rush. At the 88th minute of the match, two minutes before the end of the game, Celtic scored, making the score Rangers 0, Celtic 1.

A nerve-racking time for fans, but many thought the game was over and pressed towards the exit, down a wide flight of stairs leading out of the stadium. Hundreds surged towards the exits at the Rangers end. Suddenly there was an almighty roar from fellow supporters. Had Rangers scored the equaliser?

In this split second exited supporters about-turned and tried to make their way back up the stairs to see what had happened, to see if Rangers really had scored the equaliser. They were opposed by their own jubilant companions who were attempting to leave the stadium, realising that at this late stage it would be impossible for either side to score another goal.

A mass exodus began at infamous Gate 13 which was about to become a disaster zone for home supporters trying to get out while fellow supporters were trying to get back in. The sea of exiting supporters were unable to stop the momentum behind them as they came face to face with the returning fans. It was the equivalent of a counter-attack. Those at the rear had no idea what was happening and continued to push forwards.

Ibrox witnessed carnage that day at Gate 13. Many fell and were unable to get up as the stampede of supporters crashed over them. Sixty-six people died, all leaving devastated families.

The disaster had not been witnessed by that majority of fans on both sides who used other exits – they happily made their way home or returned to the pubs, which filled up as normal after a match.

The media were making frantic appeals on radio and television for all those who'd attended the match to make contact with their homes. Many heard the newsflashes and did so, but many remained totally oblivious and continued to party.

Back in East Kilbride the weather had deteriorated – the fog was

The aftermath of the
Ibrox disaster at Gate 13

so thick as to be unwork-
able. The shocking mag-
nitude of the disaster was
beginning to emerge as
the reported death toll
rose. It was then that I was
radioed by my control
room to pick up a lady in
distress over her son's
well-being and take her to
her family in Toryglen in
Glasgow. Her son had not
rung her, and the gate he
would have used would
have been Gate 13.

It was a desperate request I dreaded but could not ignore. On
picking up the lady I was thanked for coming out in such extreme
conditions. The fog was by this time impossibly dense, the route
virtually undriveable. And it got worse. Beyond Nerston village we
almost ground to a halt in fog like I'd never seen before. Visibility
was almost nil.

I craned head and shoulders out of my side window trying to
make out the broken white lines that marked the centre of the road
and the way to Toryglen. It seemed to take hours to descend from
East Kilbride to Rutherglen and into Toryglen.

There my passenger frantically left the cab and hammered at a
door which immediately opened, but the equally anxious relations
inside had no news either. Their desperate wait continued.

I headed home, with thick fog as my companion. Entering East
Kilbride, I received another call from the radio room. This time
it was excellent news: my passenger's son had arrived home and
could I please pass on the news to his mother that all was well.

I headed back into the fog but I was keen to return to the address in Toryglen with such great news, better news than they'd ever had before. Though the fog was just as bad, for some reason I didn't feel it took me anything like as long as the previous journey. I was sure when I passed on the news it would be received with elation.

On arriving, I knocked at the door, which was opened almost immediately by a family member desperate for good news. I explained who I was and that I had an urgent message for my passenger. She came to the door to receive the most wonderful news a mother could hear.

I don't know what I expecting, but definitely not what happened. She collapsed into my arms as I told her: 'Your son's arrived safely – he's at your home in East Kilbride.'

Sadly not all mothers and wives received such good news that evening. Many were left to cope with the realisation of their worst fears, that sons or husbands were never coming home again.

I'd sincerely love a little reunion with that unknown mother as I'll never forget my elation that day. The privilege of passing such wonderful news to someone in distress is something most people will never experience – for me it was my most beautiful moment as a taxi driver. In fact it was probably the most rewarding experience of my life.

GLASGOW ROYAL INFIRMARY GLADIATORS

One of the hospitals I go to often is the Glasgow Royal Infirmary in Castle Street, just a mile from the City Centre. It has the most central casualty department.

In the 'fifties and 'sixties Glasgow was notorious for gang warfare. Local gangs, armed with weapons and knuckle-dusters, would fight pitched battles in and around the city. They'd carve each other up with knives and hatchets, even swords. Stabbings and slashings were common and often resulted in death.

These gang fights would end in the regular conveying of the

injured from battle zone to casualty department at the Glasgow Royal Infirmary, a very experienced healing ground where they'd get stitched back together again.

So many thugs turned up at casualty that the police were in twenty-four-hour attendance, taking statements or simply keeping the peace. That way doctors and nurses felt more secure – because it could be a frightening place to work.

But of course the police presence did not always keep the peace.

When the battle was over and the injured gladiators were transported to hospital, the worst of the trouble was sometimes still to come. It was here that both gangs would meet again. As the exchange of sarcastic comments became more venomous, battle would erupt for a second time.

I witnessed several of these skirmishes in the casualty department. They were gruesome and frightening. The bloody wounds inflicted in the first fight would by this time have leaked through shirts and jackets soon to be daubed again with fresh blood – the impression was of a total bloodbath. After a counterattack the floor would be awash with blood, old and new.

After hours of repair work, the gladiators would be ready to limp homewards – and that of course is where we came in. We'd regularly be regaled with the reasons for the conflict and how hard they'd tried to avoid it – alas, it was always the other side that started it. Their frustrations, their bitterness, the parts they'd played in the battle and, of course, who did what to whom were discussed with great gusto all the way home.

The Glasgow Royal Infirmary is on the front line for City Centre incidents. The staff's experience in dealing with the badly injured is second to none, they've saved countless lives over the years.

Every warrior who's enjoyed its hospitality owes the Glasgow Royal Infirmary a huge debt of gratitude.

Did you know that the word 'taxi' is internationally recognised? The same spelling and meaning applies in almost every country. It may just be that this is the first truly international word.

FINGERS

A very good taxi-driver friend of mine, Gordon Peebles, told me about a hire he picked up at the Glasgow Cross rank.

The Glasgow Cross taxi rank

There were two men helping a third into his taxi. 'They were three Glasgow hardmen. I thought one of them was drunk, he was needing help from the other two. When they asked for the Glasgow Royal Infirmary I realised it was more serious than that.'

Blood had saturated his shirt and trousers; a pool of blood collected on the taxi floor as it sped towards the hospital. Gordon radioed his controller to warn the casualty department of our arrival through a direct link we had from our office.

On the journey there were many foul curses from all three about what had taken place. They knew the hospital would notify the police and questions would be asked. This was not what they wanted, they were used to dealing with matters themselves – police involvement was detested under any circumstances. Details of this stabbing should be known only to the people concerned.

The new Glasgow Royal Infirmary casualty department in Alexander Parade

'Don't grass,' was the decision of all three. 'We'll get him back later, just don't grass.'

The cab was by this time approaching Accident and Emergency; awaiting its arrival was a team of doctors and nurses who whisked the victim away for urgent attention. The wonderful nursing staff, who could see what a terrible state the taxi was in, with blood-soaked doors and floor awash with blood, even offered to clean up the mess.

Gordon was paid for his labour, and took off.

Several months later he again picked up one of these gents – not the victim, one of his escorts. He asked after his mate and was told he'd had a close brush with death but had survived, no problem. Details of the revenge attack were eagerly divulged:

'We managed to get him drinking in the same pub six weeks later. We grabbed him at the bar and spread his right hand out. Then we chopped his fingers off with an axe.'

THE VICTORIA SOAP DISH

The Victoria Infirmary, which serves the South Side of Glasgow, like most large hospitals has a taxi rank outside its main door. This I've frequented for thirty years.

At some point in the working day, a toilet stop is necessary for the taxi driver.

The Victoria
Infirmary
taxi rank

This is where the Victoria Infirmary comes in.

Just inside the hospital is a small paper shop, a tea room run by the WRVS (which incidentally receives not just payment for teas and sandwiches from cabbies but many little extras in appreciation of the fine work done by these women), a public telephone and, of course, a toilet.

A small toilet with a single wash-basin for which I am always grateful. My thanks to the NHS for so often saving my life in times of desperation.

But also to all those toilet attendants who for thirty years without a break have managed with impeccable dedication *never* to fill the liquid-soap holder. I'm sure this is a record for commitment and consistency.

DRUGS RUN

The unwitting taxi driver is sometimes roped into what we call a drugs run.

It starts off innocently enough. He's asked to go to an address, then to wait a few minutes. The passenger returns swiftly if no joy is to be had there and another address is given, usually just around the corner. At this point the cabbie realises his fare is on the hunt for drugs. It can take several calls before the desired substance is obtained.

It surprises me how many dealers can be located in a small area. In one drugs run in Possilpark we called at six houses in a quarter of a square mile. And that's only the ones a taxi driver gets to know about.

NOT A GOOD DAY

It was in the winter of 1978 that one of my drivers, Jimmy McDonald, just about came to the end of his tether over schoolkids pelting his cab with snowballs.

It was bad enough keeping the cab on the road in heavy snow, but the sudden thuds as snowballs thumped into the cab were shattering his nerves. He got so angry he promised himself he'd batter the next one that threw anything at him.

He didn't have long to wait. On an overhead walkway was a crowd of teenagers waiting for him to come into range. They let fly. The cab was rattled from all angles.

Jimmy skidded to a halt. The surprised kids scattered like cockroaches when the light goes on. Determined to capture at least one perpetrator, he tore after them. The chase was on.

Jimmy was a hundred yards from his cab and moving well when he heard a colossal thump from the direction of his unattended vehicle. He knew the sound and a sickening feeling hit the pit of his stomach.

He stopped in his tracks, turned about, and confirmed his worst fears. A white Ford transit van following the tracks his cab had made had failed to negotiate the slight right-hand bend just before the bridge and had slithered into the rear of the waiting taxi.

Abandoning the chase of the merry little snowballers, Jimmy headed back up the gradient towards the transit. The return journey was not as easy as the outward charge. Tired, sickened and humiliated, he was struggling towards the scene of the accident when he heard another unwelcome sound – the scream of rubber failing to grip the shiny snow. The transit was attempting a getaway.

The race was on again, this time to get back to the cab. The van managed to get to grips with the snow but the same could not be said for poor Jim. He fell, and from his humiliating horizontal position watched the offending van wriggle down the road into oblivion.

The overhead walkway again filled with an audience of smirking schoolkids as Jimmy limped back. He'd like to have bulldozed the lot of them. It had been a solid hit on the taxi cab, one that would cost him dearly.

ACCIDENT SPREE

I was working the day shift for my father in 1973 when I and my night-shift mate were given a brand new cab. HUS 834L – I still remember its registration number.

I was pleased as Punch. It was like driving a Rolls-Royce. The first day I drove about kidding on I was looking for work but really I was just getting myself noticed.

On day two in the life of my new machine the milometer read 180 miles. I'd just taken an old lady and her daughter and baby granddaughter from the South Side of Glasgow to the Dundas Street side of Queen Street station.

Dundas Street today. Before the Buchannan Galleries (in the background) were built in the 'nineties, it ran right up the hill.

I parked the cab at the back of the taxi rank at the entrance to the station and jumped out to assist my passengers. I supported one end of the pram and the mother the other, and we lifted the child gently onto the pavement. No sooner had I turned round to help the old lady than I heard an almighty bang and saw my taxi, hit from behind by a bus, fly down the street and smash into the last cab on the rank.

During this unmanned journey of my brand new cab, I witnessed the 83-year-old grandmother take flight. She flew through the air six feet from the ground and crash-landed in the gutter, then slid a further ten feet. She ended up lying under the last taxi on the rank, just before the front of my car embedded itself in that same taxi.

The ambulance came and rushed the old lady to the Glasgow Royal Infirmary. I believe she was poorly for some time, having recieved a fractured skull and extensive bruising, but to the best of my knowledge she made a full recovery.

The police took details of the accident and a statement from the offending bus driver. He blamed the wet cobbled street.

My new cab was towed away to the main agents for damage assessment. This was extensive. As there was no back boot, the bus had crunched into the body of the cab. The passenger doors were buckled, the passenger floor was like Dolly Parton on a good day. The front had also sustained a heavy hit. We needed a completely new front end with all the trimmings.

The cab could have been a write-off had it not been only two days old. It was six weeks before we got it back, a costly six weeks for both owner and driver. Then it took a full day's work to remove the dust and paint marks from the inside.

I was just back into the swing of things when I was asked to take the vehicle for its important 500-mile service. On the way to the garage I stopped at a red light and as I waited noticed in my rear-view mirror that a Glasgow Corporation Lighting Department van was approaching − rather swiftly − my recently repaired rear end.

Either I was invisible or the driver of the van wanted a fresh paint job. Bracing myself against the steering wheel and sending the brake pedal through the floor, I awaited the uninvited presence. He duly arrived, crunching my rear into what it had looked like six weeks before.

The van driver dived out of his vehicle to explain how the accident had happened. I felt I didn't need it explained in too much detail, I'd already got the drift. He'd seen his mate walking down the street a hundred yards back and was trying to attract his attention to show him he was in a new job, and he didn't notice that the traffic in front had stopped − so, guess what?

Another week, another new back end.

Glasgow Corporation at that time had an insurance office on Trongate where I became quite a familiar face, I visited them so often with accident claims.

My cab was eight weeks old with only 1,000 miles on the clock when it was returned for another complete paint job at the rear. The very next day I was travelling up Bath Street when the driver of a Corporation bus turned into Wellington Street without looking and ripped the side of my cab along both doors and the rear wing.

A bashed FX4 being towed off

Apologies from the driver, he'd forgotten about turning until the last second.

Back to the body shop.

Back to the insurance office.

A TX1 cab being repaired after an accident

Another week off the road. Buying a new cab doesn't always solve all the problems. The situation was serious, too much time had been lost. Grabbing the odd shift here and there was completely inadequate.

We thought the jinx had left us when we got the cab back and worked uninterruptedly for about two weeks. That was until my night-shift mate met the same fate as me at 3,000 miles.

He was stationary at a set of traffic lights on Cathcart Road when, believe it or not, another Corporation van ploughed into the twice-rebuilt back end.

Back again to the body shop.

Back again to the insurance office.

Yet another week off the road.

The rest of the car's history was uneventful, we were allowed to work steadily after that. No more smashing times!

Did you know that almost all of Glasgow's taxis use diesel fuel, not petrol, and that this is *dearer* than petrol by one or two pence per litre?

DOOR HANDLES

Modern customer-friendly cabs allow passengers ease of entry with exterior door handles that are simple to operate.

This was not always the case. The old pull-down and push-button handles were stiff and often required the driver to leave his cab to help passengers gain entry.

Unless, of course, the rain was bouncing off the streets and every passenger was desperate for shelter, then every one of them managed to open those doors with ease.

I wonder why?

COLD COMFORT

I'm always amazed at the number of people who enter my cab and with great delight start describing their cold or flu symptoms.

There'll follow proof in the form of uncontrolled fits of coughing and spluttering. Sneezing six or seven times also helps convince the driver that his passenger is in need of sympathy.

Does none of them ever think about the poor driver?

He's in the front line, four feet away, in the direct line of fire from airborne spray with nowhere to go but in his direction. Some sufferers will actually change seats during a performance, pulling down the bucket seat so they can get close enough for a direct hit.

It's specially worrying if someone indicates he's just back from the Congo …

Ah yes, in true Glasgow spirit our passengers like to share everything with us.

OVERSPENT

I thought I'd heard just about every excuse from passengers with no money wanting a free lift home, but there's always one more.

I was hailed by a lady on Queen Margaret Drive in the West End who confided that she'd overspent at the shops so had no money but please could I take her home and get paid at the other end as she'd just started to menstruate and she had a fungal infection.

That deserved a run home. What a beauty – imagine saying that!

AT GUNPOINT

I've only once in all my driving years had the misfortune to have a handgun pulled on me.

Luckily it was a joke, the gun a toy replica. I know the young man holding it meant me no harm, and expected me to share his joke.

My mind went totally blank. I can't remember what he said when he pointed the gun in my face. I had an idea it might be a fake, but I didn't know for certain.

You may think that in that situation you could spot the difference between a real gun and a replica, but I can assure you your mind goes into hyperdrive and you doubt the obvious. Until you find yourself in that position you don't know how you'll react. But I'll hazard a guess – you'll need a change of underwear just like me!

THE EASTERHOUSE SNORER

Around 4am one Sunday morning my son Gordon was having difficulty waking a male passenger from an exceedingly deep sleep.

Wanting to get home from the City Centre after a Saturday night binge, the man had asked to be taken to Easterhouse. The exact address was still unknown ... so efforts had to be made to awaken the snorer.

All the usual methods were tried to get him to surface:

- Throwing the cab from side to side to jerk him back to life.
- Braking suddenly to throw him onto the cab floor, hopefully to awaken and wonder where he was.
- Shouting at him through the intercom that he was home.
- Adding that if he didn't wake up and collect his change it was going into the driver's pocket.

All the above failed to have any effect. Gordon was going to have to stop the cab and give him a shake. This would have to be done very carefully. It was known for passengers to come out of a drunken stupor thinking they were being assaulted in the bar they'd just left. The poor driver could then be on the receiving end of frantic punches. This didn't happen in this case. The Big Sleep continued.

Gordon was running out of time. He needed to hand the cab over to the day-shift driver and this 'change-over' was fast approaching. The cab first had to be taken through the taxi car-wash. He decided to go straight there in the hope that in all the activity his sleeper would surface.

The cab joined the car-wash queue and was dealt with while its driver had a cup of tea and a blether with the other the cabbies. Another attempt was then made to awaken the Easterhouse Snorer but the result was the same as before.

'This guy was solid gone.'

However, as the inside of a taxicab is all made of washable

materials, it was possible to turn the car-wash hose on him at full blast – with more interesting results.

He sprang to life screaming and cursing. Leaping out of the cab to find himself surrounded by taxi drivers, his first thought must have been that he'd taken on the whole of the Glasgow cab trade.

But all the drivers were laughing at him so he must soon have wondered just what the hell was going on.

Dripping from top to bottom, he decided not to push his luck. He sauntered off in the first direction available, with an audible squelch from his footwear.

Probably all the way to Easterhouse ...

THE DOMESTIC DISPUTE

In these days of zero tolerance, cab drivers don't see the same number of violent domestic incidents as they once did. Domestic violence used to be very visible on the streets of Glasgow, and especially around closing time a husband-and-wife battle was a regular sight.

It often took place in the taxi as both parties were being taken home. It wasn't uncommon for a wife to enter a cab smiling and leave a few minutes later with her face battered and bleeding.

It's easy to say a driver should have done something to stop the abuse, but this is usually impossible. A taxi driver, unlike a policeman, has no legal authority to exert force. And he's not a qualified go-between, so doesn't have the respect of either party.

I was warned many times by old cabbies never to get involved in a domestic dispute, it would almost certainly backfire on me. Many drivers have tried to stop a husband from beating up his wife and most end up telling a similar tale.

If a driver tries to separate the two parties the man (usually the aggressor, often fuelled with alcohol) will turn on him in turn. A very violent exchange of blows can be the result.

As the driver is sober and his opponent usually is not, he will eventually start to get the better of the situation. At this point the wife, seeing her husband being struck by a stranger, will come to his rescue. So she joins the fight. The driver now has to battle with two people.

In the end the warring partners will head for home hand-in-hand, licking their wounds, having found common ground. They'll discuss how the bad taxi driver was totally out of order...

The moral of the story is don't get involved.

HARD-EARNED WAGES

It was around 7.30pm one Friday evening that I picked up a young mother in the Milton scheme of North Glasgow. Before entering the cab she said goodbye to her 8-year-old daughter and promised she'd be back shortly.

It was a strange pick-up. The daughter was crying for her mother to stay though it was clear she knew she had to go.

'I'll be back soon. Look after the baby. I'll be back soon, don't fret.'

She instructed me to take her to the Glen Douglas bar in Balmore

The Glen Douglas bar

Road, just about five minutes away. It was the local Milton bar, a favourite stop-off for working men on their way home. My passenger said she'd only be five minutes, please could I wait and take her home again. She seemed to be frightened.

When we arrived she took a deep breath and went inside. About two minutes later she reappeared, escorted by a man who turned out to be her husband. She was arguing with him, looking for him to give her money.

He produced what looked like a wage packet and extracted a bundle of notes. The mother examined them and satisfied herself as to amount she'd been given.

I was trying to make out what they were arguing about but could only hear him asking over and over if she was satisfied with the amount from the wage packet.

'Yes! Yes! Yes!' she replied. 'That's what I wanted last week as well, but you drank it!'

He let fly with a right-handed power punch straight into her face, which sent her crashing to the ground, then began yelling at her as she lay there nursing her bleeding face. I'll never forget his words:

'Now yu've got yer wages, don't ever come into the pub and embarrass me in front of my mates again! Get yurself hame and look after the kids. That's where yi belong.'

He finished the verbal dressing-down everyone around could hear then casually returned to his mates in the pub. She picked herself up from the pavement and returned to the cab.

She told me both she and her child of 8 had known she'd be going to the pub for a sore face. It was the only way her husband could keep the respect of the other men – she had to be punished for 'taking him down'. But going to the pub was the only way she could get any money to feed the family for the week ahead. Otherwise all the wages would have disappeared that night.

The daughter, watching for us, came running out in tears with arms wide open to share her mother's pain. I realised that for some families this was a weekly occurrence, this was how some women had to pay for their housekeeping money.

MY FIRST £100 FARE

One evening around Christmas time some years ago I picked up a lady in the City Centre after an office party.

She'd had a good evening but was very upset about being transferred from the Glasgow office to London. She'd have to move house and she wasn't happy.

I sympathised but said these things happen sometimes, it's probably unavoidable.

'No!' was the sharp reply. 'It's quite avoidable and unnecessary!'

She explained that she and her boss had been sleeping together and the boss's wife had found out and insisted that she be sacked or moved to London.

At her destination she asked me to wait. She returned five minutes later and, to my delight, asked me to take her another twenty-five miles. We arrived around 1.30am and here she again asked me to wait, this time for only two minutes. She returned happy and full of smiles.

'Now take me home, driver,' she said joyfully.

I could smell a fish. Although I was delighted at the prospect of another twenty-five-mile journey, the estimated fare now being around £50, I knew something was not adding up.

Curiosity was getting the better of me. I asked her why she'd go to all the expense of hiring a cab to take her twenty-five miles there and twenty-five miles back and only stop off for two minutes.

Happily she told me that in her house she'd had a spare shirt and tie belonging to her boss; we'd just left her boss's house, where she'd wrapped the shirt round the windscreen wipers of the wife's car and the tie round the door handle.

'Obviously she'll recognise his things in the morning. All hell will break loose!'

I tried to persuade her it was just the drink making her do this and that we could easily redeem the situation by going back and recovering the items. Her reply was very bitter – I was to take her home. My pleas for her to reconsider were brushed aside. She was unrepentant, she wanted to go home.

I gave up trying to change her mind. I got her home at 2.30am – when she was suddenly struck with remorse.

'Driver,' she said sheepishly, 'please take me back for the shirt and tie. I've plenty of money for the fare. Please take me back.'

Another fifty miles later, at about 4.30am, we were back at her house for the third time, having completed the recovery process, boss and lady wife none the wiser.

The fare totalled £100 and she gave me a £10 tip. A lot of money to go nowhere.

Did you know that, when he's about to finish a lengthy journey, the best words a cab driver can hear are, 'Is it possible to wait five minutes and then take me back again?'

THE HAMILTON TOW ROPE

It was 1971 and I was driving a taxi in East Kilbride, an old Austin Cambridge, a great workhorse in its day.

I went to Hamilton to help another driver who'd broken down in a Ford Zephyr Mark III. Chick was very despondent. His car had been off the road all week for an engine rebuild, this was a busy Friday night and it looked as if his plans to recoup lost wages had been scuppered.

After trying unsuccessfully to find the fault, we bought a tow rope and tried to start the car by towing it. No joy. So we decided to tow it back to East Kilbride.

It was 10.15pm and the pubs were busy clearing drinkers out of their establishments – they closed their doors at 10 o'clock in those days.

I was towing the Zephyr downhill towards a set of traffic lights where we had to turn left for East Kilbride. The lights were against us so we stopped. Immediately in front of us was that famous

Hamilton landmark, Skeltons Bar. Outside it a closing-time drunk was supporting a lamppost, waiting to cross the road. He was well dressed in a suit and a fine pair of highly polished shoes. I remember thinking him most unusual, far above the usual quality of punter coming out of Skeltons at 10.15pm.

The lights changed and I set off, watching the gentleman as I turned left to make sure he wasn't going to dart between our two cars and trip over our brand new rope. Then I started to accelerate towards the approaching hill. As I did this I felt the car at the back suddenly jolt badly. My first thought was that Chick was trying to bump start it again. I changed my mind when I heard the screams of girls on the pavement.

Realising that my drunk gent had after all made a last-second dash across the road between our cars, only to trip, I braked hard and leapt out of the car. Almost simultaneously Chick shot out of the Zephyr. He'd braked violently on seeing the man fall over but then released the brake so that the front wheel could roll over him without causing too much damage.

We both surveyed our helpless friend underneath the Zephyr, between the front and rear wheels. Relief was immediately at hand from the local cavalry just released from Skeltons Bar. Without instruction, almost by telepathy, everyone bent down, gripped the car beneath the sill on one side and ... one, two, three ... lifted it up so that our drunk could be hauled out and laid out on the pavement.

Ten seconds of recovery time later he stood up, his suit in tatters, looking like it had been through a shredder. He himself seemed in perfect condition and, to my amazement, now totally sober. I have never seen anyone sober up that quickly in all my life.

The police arrived and thoroughly checked both our vehicles but said no charges would be brought. The new tow rope had come with the appropriate warning tag to alert pedestrians.

Our drunken friend was whisked away in an ambulance for a check-up. He must have been okay as we heard nothing more about the incident.

Did you know that foreigners are often surprised Glasgow taxis can carry five passengers? When they find out they'll pile in, three on the back seat, two sitting on the floor! It's a laugh when you point out the two pull-down seats for the low-down bums.

ARE YOU SITTING COMFORTABLY?

Sometimes people entering the taxicab will still be waving goodbye to friends. They forget they're not getting into a private car and attempt to sit down before they've reached the back seat. This results in a clatter and a bang and an embarrassed passenger lying flat on the floor.

Never in any circumstances must the driver have a wee chuckle.

Did you know that as long as the driver keeps his foot on the brake pedal the doors are locked so it's impossible for a passenger to exit the cab without paying the fare?

BAIRD STREET POLICE STATION

About 2am one Sunday morning a male nightclub reveller jumped into the cab at Charing Cross and asked me to take him to Duke Street in Dennistoun.

We were just at the entrance to the motorway heading east so I got onto it and came off at the exit for Dennistoun, just short of my passenger's destination.

'Ah see yur takin' me the lang wie,' came a coarse voice from the back. 'Yur getin' nae f**kin' money aff me fur this journey, no' ah f**kin' penny.'

I tried to explain that this route was the shortest. To no avail. Nothing I said could convince him.

'No' ah f**kin penny ur yi gettin'. Take me ti the polis station.'

Baird Street police station struggle to cope with demand at peak times.

I realised I wasn't winning this one so drove to Baird Street police station. I could see they were having a wonderful night. The queue was about twenty people long. They were even queuing up outside, waiting for their disputes to be resolved. It was just that time of night when the police can't cope with demand. I pressed my horn, hoping to draw the attention of officers at the bar, but the din created by the gaggle of geese outside drowned me out.

After a few minutes my agitated passenger asked if it'd be alright for him to leave the cab, go inside and try to persuade the officer at the bar to let us jump the queue. My foot was on the brake pedal, which prevented him from leaving – he was effectively locked in. I suggested that if I let him out that would be the last I'd see of him. He and his cash would be in Dennistoun in jig time and I'd have lost my £5 fare and be left looking like an idiot.

'Aw naw, driver, Ah'm no' runnin' aff wi' yur money, Ah'm wan o' the guid guys. Here, ho'd own ti ma tenner an' Ah'll go in an' git them.'

I accepted it with delight. After trying the door, he turned back to me and asked me to release the lock and let him out. I assured him the doors were now released as I handed him his change from the amount shown on the meter.

He realised what he'd done and obviously felt like a turkey. The journey cost him £2 more than it would have if we'd made a straight run to Dennistoun – and he still had a mile to walk from the police station.

THE NOISY GEARBOX

While our cab was off the road for repair my night-shift driver and I hired another taxi. It was due to be replaced and the fleet owner hadn't wanted to spend money on it for the short life it had left.

The gearbox was noisy at the start. Towards the end of the week it was deafening, denying passengers any conversation with the driver. A hire to Tollcross Road in the East End wasn't impressed when he asked the driver to stop at the next junction and the driver carried on. He became quite upset when a second request was ignored as the cab flew past his destination. Infuriated when his fourth or fifth request was denied, he lunged at the driver and grabbed him by the throat. The cab came to a halt.

That was the last shift that my night-shift man worked in that vehicle. His nerves were as shattered as his eardrums.

THE BOLTER

An experienced driver can usually smell trouble as it enters the cab. And sometimes just before.

This day I picked up a young gent who asked me to take him to Hamilton. I was sure something was not quite right. At the destination the passenger door burst open and he bolted into oblivion.

Even worse than losing the money is being left to kick yourself for not trusting your instincts. I knew I should've asked him for payment up front.

I was soon back in my working area, where my next passenger handed me a wallet he found lying on the floor. To my delight I realised it belonged to the bolter and contained his ID with photograph – would you believe it, he worked at Glasgow Airport!

Armed with the evidence, I went to the police station. My money for the fare was ready for collection next day.

THE CHEAPEST ROUTE

To keep the fare to a minimum I always try to take the shortest route, but sometimes two routes are almost equidistant and I
argue with myself over which is best.

Then I usually give the passenger the choice, describing both to
him. That way he can't complain at the end of the journey.

However, given this choice, 95% of travellers will simply reply,
'The cheapest one.'

Fine!

Did you know that not all taxi ranks keep the same hours?
There are many throughout the city – at busy junctions, hospitals,
shopping centres, train and bus stations – and most operate both
day and night, depending of course on the availability of cabs and
on demand. But not all work on a 24-hour basis. The one outside
the Garage nightclub in Sauchiehall Street (some of us remember
this area better as the location of Locarno ballroom) only operates
from early evening until 6am, serving all the night-time pubgoers,
clubbers and gamblers on this lively stretch of road. The rank inside
Queen Street station operates from 6am until midnight, when cars
transfer to the rank at North Hanover Street and George Square to
serve night-time revellers trying to get home.

THE STRANGLER CABLE

The early FX4s of the 'sixties and 'seventies were fitted with
a stop cable that, when pulled, cut the fuel supply to the engine and
stopped the vehicle immediately. It was a standard feature for a diesel
engine and was known as the strangler cable.

The ignition key started the vehicle but, if the strangler cable was
pulled out and kept in the stop position, the vehicle wouldn't start.
It would go through the motions of starting, turning the engine
over, but it wouldn't fire up.

This could be very useful, especially to a night-shift driver who picked up undesirable passengers who asked to be taken to outlying areas of ill repute. The odds in such a case are stacked against the cabbie so that it's better for him to carry on with the fare than to stop and try to force the rowdies out.

It became a standing joke for a driver to pull out the strangler cable while the cab was in motion so that it immediately cut out and ground to a halt. He could then apologise to his passengers and say he'd had the fault rectified only last week and thought it had gone away. He'd ask them to get out and push to get the cab started again, then he'd take them to their destination completely free of charge. With this promise the rowdies always got out and pushed.

After a few yards the driver would push the strangler cable back home, engage gear, let the clutch out and jolt the engine back into life. The revellers would stop pushing and watch in dismay as he waved them goodbye.

TRAILER WHEELS

At the Righead roundabout in East Kilbride, one of my drivers stopped in the line of traffic.

Awaiting his turn to go through, he observed a 32-ton articulated lorry approaching from another direction and was amazed to see that the rear wheels of the trailer had come off and were heading straight for him, bouncing over the pavements.

True to form, they crashed straight into my vehicle, causing extensive damage on the driver's side. He immediately radioed the control room and alerted the other thirty cabs in East Kilbride to stop the southbound artic.

Surely it would be a doddle – thirty cabs seeking one articulated lorry heading for the M74 with its two rear trailer wheels missing? But after half an hour's extensive search we concluded it must be well on its way towards the border, minus its two trailer wheels and probably with a driver laughing his head off.

HONEST DICK

All through my taxi days my old mate Dick Brown and I have been close friends. Dick is as honest as the day is long. We share the same cab: I work days and Dick is on the night shift.

Very early one weekend morning, around 4am as the casinos started to empty, Dick was asked by a customer to take him to the outskirts of Glasgow. A little concerned that the man had consumed his fair share of the laughing fluid and might not have money to pay the fare, Dick told him that the cost of the hire would be £12.

'Ah, driver, money is no problem! I just had a wee win in the casino. Do you think I have enough cash here to cover the fare?' He waved aloft a huge bundle of banknotes, obviously a lot more than was needed.

On reaching his destination, Dick advised him to make sure he had all his money with him, that he hadn't dropped any on the floor or seat. To make sure his passenger wasn't going to be out of pocket, Dick opened the door for him and checked the cab.

After driving away, Dick felt the need to reassure himself once more that no money could have been left in the back. Again he checked the cab. Nothing.

But then he noticed that the bucket seat was not quite flat. Upon investigating, a roll of notes fell with a soft thud onto the floor. It was a staggering £600 of the casino winner's cash.

The rear-facing bucket seats where the £600 was found

113

A trip back to the drop-off point proved fruitless, so Dick handed the cash in at a police station. Now that's an honest cabbie!

He later received a letter from them saying that, as the cash had not been claimed, he was now the worthy winner of £600.

Did you know that the improved interior design of the new TX1 and Metrocab allows the rear seat armrest to be converted into a baby seat so that small children can be carried in safety, in compliance with legal requirements? Young mothers take note! Travel safely with your child in a Real Taxi.

THE SUPERNATURAL

My father and I were talking one day about taxi work and the situations that arise from time to time. It was about 1972, when I was driving an old Austin Cambridge in East Kilbride. I told him about a weird thing that had happened the week before.

It started at exactly 11.50pm on a fine summer's evening, after I picked up a young lady at the town centre taxi rank. She'd just got off the late-night bus from Glasgow. She asked politely to be taken to Strathaven, a small village eight miles away, in the middle of nowhere.

We set off and were soon in the countryside, no other vehicles in sight. East Kilbride taxi drivers used to know that as soon as they leave the East Kilbride boundary, heading for Strathaven, they'd lose contact with the radio room and be on their own. No further contact would be possible until they were back within the perimeter of the town.

The Strathaven road was known to be lonely and desolate, particularly at that time of night. On this occasion a full moon glistened eerily as we made our way deep into the countryside.

I checked my watch. It had just gone 11.55. If all went well, I'd be dropping my passenger off about ten minutes past midnight.

The full moon and midnight seemed to be sending me messages.

The full moon ... and midnight ... A lonely and desolate road ... My mind was spinning. It was two minutes to midnight.

We were approaching a straight stretch of road where the way ahead in the moonlight would be clear for a mile and a half. If I saw the road ahead was deserted I'd be convinced it was only my mind playing tricks ...

But on entering the straight section I could see a set of headlamps shining from the far end. It was midnight. As I checked my watch the full moon above sent shivers down my spine. I seemed to be gliding towards the motionless headlights unable to slow down in case I struck fear into the heart of my unsuspecting passenger.

I glanced over my shoulder at her to reassure myself that all was well, and met her anxious eyes. Had she noticed the time, the moon, the headlights ... ?

I was by now convinced that the lights of the other vehicle showed no sign of flickering or bumping up and down. The car was stationary. Why would a car stop on this lonely stretch of road? I was conscious of my own car's speed – I wanted to slow down but couldn't bear to dent my macho image with my young lady looking on.

I could now make out that the stationary vehicle was slumped to one side. Had it run off the road into a ditch? I couldn't take my eyes off the road ahead but sensed something was about to happen. Something inside me was shouting, *Soon, very soon.*

My foot eased off the accelerator – to hell with the macho image, fear had overtaken me. Suddenly a huge man loomed up in the middle of the road. I hadn't seen him from a distance as he was all in black. A long black trench coat draped his body, he had black footwear and long black hair supported by a thick dark growth on his face.

He looked about seven feet tall, and he was slowly beckoning me to stop with a waving motion of his outstretched albatross arms. The word *werewolf* boomed in my terrified mind as if from a clock striking midnight. The full moon was laughing at me for being a confessed unbeliever before.

Werewolf. It was obvious. The figure in front of me was assuming its midnight form, just as the full moon demanded.

Werewolf. Good God it's a werewolf!

I glanced over at the stationary vehicle and could clearly see two passengers sitting in an upright position. What were they *doing* just *sitting* there? Could they not move out of the car? Were they dead? Had he just killed them?

This was not normal.

I was almost upon him, my speed reduced to a limp tick-over. Time to lock the doors. A quick glance behind me revealed my white-faced companion staring terrifyingly at me, trusting me, knowing both our lives depended on my judgement. Distance zeroed in as we came close to the paranormal aparition.

He was obviously wanting to talk to me, leaning forward. I rolled the window down an inch or two, just enough for him to pass a verbal message, not enough for an arm or a hand. Attack might be imminent.

I felt isolated, with no radio link, no other possibility of contact. The hackles on the back of my neck were at screaming point. My left foot was riding the clutch; the accelerator pedal would be floored in an instant if ...

The hairy dark face was lowered towards me.

Oh God! This is it!

'C-c-co-cou-could you...?' The deep voice stuttered badly, the change from man to werewolf must be well on the way ...

'C-c-co-cou-could you telephone Strathaven Police...?'

Is this really it?

'C-c-co-cou-could you telephone Strathaven Police a-an-and tell them...?'

My heart almost stopped. What sort of grisly admission would come at midnigt from a werewolf?

'...I'm a policeman, I'm taking prisoners from Strathaven police station to Barlinnie prison and I've broken down. Could you help me please by asking them to come to my rescue?'

I acknowledged the request and took off. Calming relief began to seep through into my explosive mind boggling with its self-inflicted nightmare.

One I'd not like to repeat.

No matter how silly it looks in the cold light of day, in the comfort of my own armchair, the weird circumstances of that night brought a terror that will remain with me all my years.

My father acknowledged my experience with a total understanding of the way the mind can run riot. It wasn't the response I'd expected from him. He went on to relate his own story.

One night in Springburn he picked up a hire wishing to go to Bishopbriggs. At that time the three-mile-long road to Bishopbriggs was, after the brightly-lit Springburn road, a lonely, uninhabited cobbled trail.

Midway on his journey he noticed someone on the other side of the road with an outstretched arm, as if trying to hail his cab. He thought he'd let him know he'd be returning soon, after dropping his hire, so could pick him up then.

Paying him as much attention as he could as he drove past, he was apalled to see his would-be passenger was in fact none other than … Lucifer himself!

Elation at the thought of a return fare from Bishopbriggs, unheard of at that time, was transformed into a driver's worst nightmare. Totally convinced that Lucifer was waiting for him on the return journey, my father lingered several minutes after he'd been paid off.

Trying not to let his head run riot, he fought to convince himself that an innocent lonely mortal out there was simply stranded in no-man's-land, seeking help to get him to his destination. The fact that the man was wearing a long cape had tricked my father into making the dreadful comparison.

Leaving Bishopbriggs, he'd made up his mind that, if the weird traveller was still there wanting a cab, he'd stop and pick him up.

Having cleared his mind, my father soon reached the section of dark road where he'd seen the cloaked figure. He was still there. He was in exactly the same spot as before. His arm was again outstretched, hailing the cab. Shivers froze my father's back as he gazed at the hooded traveller. *It was the Grim Reaper!* The old FX3 had almost ground to a halt...

It was the face of death!

If he let *that thing* into the taxi, one thing was certain – he would not be returning home to his family that night.

His vehicle shot forwards, towards the comfort of the bright lights of Springburn.

With Bishopbriggs behind him, having reached the safety of the Glasgow boundary just short of Springburn, he took a well-earned break at the roadside. After about five minutes a young gent chapped the window. Was the driver was available to take another fare?

'Yes, sir! ... Where would you like to go?'

'Bishopbriggs please,' came the dreaded reply.

The cab turned and headed back. This time the driver was really scared, scared right down to his boots. All he could hope for was that *the thing* had moved on... that the road was clear...

This was not to be.

He stood in the same spot, still waving, the look of death beneath his cape. A shriek was heard as the taxi flew past.

The return journey would be the worst. The fare received, as if by remote control the cab turned and headed back into *the Grim Reaper's lair*... This time my father had no intention of stopping. Straight home! Work was over for the night!

All he had to do was pass *Death* on the way home.

There he was, unmoved, but unlike before he stood in the middle of the road, both arms outstretched, defying the cab not to stop. The death mask lurked beneath the hooded cape. No mistake this time...

This was the very Devil himself.

If he stopped, he would die!

My father swerved violently off the road in a frantic attempt to avoid his adversary. Another violent swerve brought the vehicle back onto the road. This time the apparition was in his rear-view mirror.

Home ... just home!

THE ROOKIE

Every trade welcomes newcomers in a different way.

When I left Hyndland School at 16, I worked for a building contractor for a full day before realising clerical work was not for me. There they told me to call at the downstairs office and ask for a 'long stand'. Luckily I'd been warned about this (along with the left-handed screwdriver and tin of tartan paint).

Such pranks were usually sprung on youngsters just out of school but taxi drivers had to be 21 so it was assumed that they were already wise to this sort of nonsense. But a good taxi controller had many clever little tricks up his sleeve. He could usually spring a welcome to a newcomer by establishing his location and, if he was anywhere near Glasgow Zoo, send him there to ask for 'Mr C. Lion'. That would give a couple of hundred drivers out there a little chuckle while the rookie waited in vain for his hire.

The controller usually got away with it. Many a rookie didn't see the joke until months later he heard it turned on another fall guy.

Did you know that despite the cost of a new cab being in excess of £30,000, there is nowhere in the driver's compartment for thim to put his change?

APRIL FOOL

On April 1st a few years ago I dropped a hire in Achamore Road, Drumchapel. He paid me off and left the cab and I sat sorting out my money so that the notes were not mixed up.

A young man knocked on my window. I pulled it down and he apologised for disturbing me. Polite, I thought. How could I help?

He showed me a £20 note and asked if I could change it for him. As I was in the middle of sorting out my takings it was no problem. I took the note from him. It was a brand new – crisp; I held it between my front teeth while still juggling with my money.

I was going to slip the £20 note into the back of the bundle of other notes when I'd finished sorting them on my lap but, to save time for my polite friend, while still gritting it between my teeth I handed him two tenners.

He thanked me, accepting the tenners with his right hand, and at the same time snatched the £20 note from my mouth with his left. In an instant he was running like a hare into his own territory, never to be seen again.

April Fool!

TWO SOCIAL SECURITY PUNTERS

On picking up a couple of shifty looking characters, I got the impression, as I always do in such circumstances, that they might cause trouble or try to abscond with the fare – if they had money for the fare in the first place.

Extra vigilant, I tried to listen to the conversation without appearing to do so, fearing I might be on the receiving end of something undesirable. I needn't have worried. No consideration was given to the fact that I might have been listening. I could have been the proverbial fly on the wall.

Each was vying for best position in the conversation by proving he was cleverest at milking the social security system. I listened with glee as each described how he'd obtained cash in the form of a 'crisis loan'. As both had won at that game it was clear neither was 'out in front' in this first section. (Having their rent paid by the 'social' was of course taken for granted and never mentioned.)

I listened as the debate continued.

'Ah managed tay git a new cooker alang wi' a fridge fur ma hoose,' said one to the other.

'Well, Ah managed tay git a new bed an' some pots 'n' pans,' rejoined the other, 'an' Big Charlie geed mi fifty quid fur them – Ah hud a brulient weekend.'

The stalemate continued as both tried to look the biggest winner until the question of 'buroo' money came up.

'Di yi git the extra £20 own tap eh yur buroo fur bein' registered an alcoholic?'

'Aye, Ah've hud that fur years – oh, aye! Ah've hud that fur years noo.'

I was surprised – shocked even – at the last bid to win the debate.

'Ah bet yi, yi don' git what Ah git own tap eh yur brew money an' yur alcohol money...'

'Naw, Ah don' git any mair on tap... How? Whit day you git?' This was said with a frown, sceptically waiting to hear about what he'd been done out of – he thought he knew every trick in the book.

Watching in the rear-view mirror I saw the chest of our competition winner fill with pride as he realised victory was his. He was about to crucify his opponent with earth-shattering information only he had been privileged to obtain.

'Ah git an extra £22.20 a week own tap eh ma buroo money fur fresh fruit allowance.'

I won't say it.

A PLAIN BROWN PAPER PACKAGE

I received a call to pick up at a huge mansion in one of Glasgow's most salubrious suburbs.

The lady and gent, dressed in the best of designer wear, approached me with several fine-quality suitcases in matching colours. They asked me to take them to the airport as they were on their way to Switzerland.

On completing the journey, I loaded their four fine suitcases onto a trolley. The lady carefully placed a brown paper package on top of them so that her hands were free to get into her purse for the cab fare.

Mother nature then produced a small gust of wind which blew the brown paper package to the ground.

'Oh no!' she cried, 'That's my square-sliced sausage and my black pudding! I don't want anything to happen to them!'

We're all Jock Tamson's bairns.

THE COMMOTION AT LEWIS'S

One day I picked up a radio job from Netherlee, just outside Glasgow to the south. My hire was a businessman going to the old Lewis's department store in Argyle Street.

We'd just been given an emergency 10% fare increase by the powers that be at the City of Glasgow Council to cover escalating fuel costs but, although authorised, this rise didn't show on the taximeter. Instead notices had been placed prominently in all cabs to warn passengers of the increase.

My passenger said he was a stranger in town, he hadn't been to Glasgow before, so could I please point out any landmarks on our way to Lewis's. I made a special effort to make him feel welcome. I talked about Glasgow and pointed out Hampden Park and the famous Gorbals district. I even made a small detour to point out Glasgow Cross and tell him about the public hangings that used to take place there.

I was feeling quite proud of myself by the time we reached our destination, knowing our visitor had established an excellent rapport with his cab driver and would leave the city with a richer knowledge and pleasant memories which hopefully he'd share with others.

Being a typical cabbie, I thought he might possibly reward my efforts with a small gratuity. That would be a welcome indication of his appreciation of my efforts, of my *experience*.

Arriving in Argyle Street, I drove towards the central entrance of the department store so that I could point out Queen Street and the railway station at the top, this being his point of departure.

The traffic was very heavy as it was a Saturday afternoon and shoppers were out in force for the sales. I was hoping to make a quick getaway from the drop-off point so as not cause an unnecessary hold-up.

When we stopped, the meter read £4.50 – with the extra 10% this was up to £4.95. I was really disappointed when I was handed a £5 note, and even more so when my passenger waited for his 5p change. He received this in exactly five 1p pieces.

He thanked me and opened the door to get out.

Gutted, I turned away from him to put the vehicle into gear. Next thing I knew, he'd sat back down on the edge of the seat and was going through his briefcase, which was on the floor, muttering about his house keys.

Motorists at my rear were not as patient as I was – they were by this time blasting their horns in frustration. Time had come for the nice driver to say something.

'Come on mate, hurry up, get out, you're holding up the traffic!'

'It's not *me* holding up the traffic, it's *you*,' he retorted indignantly.

I saw red. *After all I've done for him!*

'I'll move the cab all right,' I said aloud.

This piece of shit sitting in the back has pushed me to the limit!

The cab lurched forward as my over-eager left foot released the clutch. The bonnet rose, the rear of the cab sank, in response to my angry demand for instant motion. It was at this point in take-off that I realised the near-side passenger door was still open. Hordes of shoppers were milling about outside the giant store.

Automatically my right foot leapt from the accelerator and slammed onto the brake. The cab nose-dived and stopped dead.

One minute my passenger had been sitting on the edge of the back seat, raking in his briefcase for his house keys, the next, as the cab had lurched forward, he'd been thrown back into the seat, his legs in the air. Now, as I hit the brake pedal, the open passenger door banged shut and a preview of what was about to happen darted through my head.

No! Please no!

But my predictions were spot on.

My passenger shot out of his seat as his legs came down and pivoted his body towards me. There was nothing I could do as I watched his face slam into the glass partition between us. His features pressed and distorted against the smooth surface of the glass and filled me with horror.

Not for his pain (I thought he deserved that) but for the conse-
quences for me. I could see the newspaper headlines screaming out
the name of the bloodthirsty taxi driver who'd assaulted an innocent visiting businessman.

The distorted face slid down the glass till the body landed with
a thump on the floor. Droves of shocked shoppers were agog at the
episode unfolding before their eyes. The crowd was so dense it was
like a Scotland v England match at Hampden Park. Not a square inch
of pavement to be seen between onlookers.

On automatic pilot I found myself opening my door and shuf-
fling round the cab to my stunned passenger, ranting as I went to
convince the crowd I was the injured party.

Opening the passenger door to reveal the body of my injured
customer twitching back to life, I began to yell at him, 'You don't
open the taxi door till the vehicle's stopped!'

I stood like a sentry guard, holding the door wide open, awaiting my customer's exit. He was battered and bewildered and all at
sea. He didn't seem to know what country he was in, never mind
where he was going or what had befallen him.

He grappled with the safety straps and levered himself slowly onto
the pavement, stunned and disorientated. The crowd of shoppers
had surely seen many a drunk man staggering out of a taxi, this was
nothing new to them.

I was beginning to think I'd got away with my little stunt and
relief was seeping back into my body, when, to my disbelief, the
crowd began to part and open up a passage for the dizzy traveller.
This passage was about ten feet wide and stretched from the cab to
the main door at Lewis's. I couldn't help thinking of the film *The
Ten Commandments*, the parting of the waters to allow safe passage
for the Jews fleeing Egypt.

But then I began to get the impression that everyone was on my
side. If he was just another drunk, the angry driver must be in the
right. No one wanted to be associated with him. That's why they
were giving him a wide berth.

I was never so pleased to see anyone disappear into a crowd.

As I made my way back to the driver's door of the cab, women were patting me on the back — forget the nasty man, have a better day from here on!

For the next few days I waited nervously for a complaint to be made against me. Sure enough, the following Wednesday I was summoned to the presence of the almighty Hackney police.

Had I taken a hire from Netherlee to Lewis's last Saturday?

'Yes… If you like I'll start at the beginning and tell you my side of the story — you've obviously heard his side.'

'Continue,' said the investigating policeman.

I began telling them exactly what I've written here. Towards the end both officers were bursting themselves laughing. I couldn't understand why. This was a serious matter.

The mirth continued until I reached the end of my tale (omitting only that the vehicle had actually stopped before the door was opened — I'm not that stupid).

'Do you smoke, John?' the officer asked.

'Only an odd cigar.'

'Well, your customer from Netherlee didn't mention anything about what you've told us, he only complained you were smoking a cigar. You know you're not allowed to smoke in the cab while carrying a fare-paying passenger, don't you John?'

'Of course.'

'However, you've made our day here,' he chuckled. 'It was quite dull until you arrived…'

He added, 'Consider yourself reprimanded for smoking with a passenger on board.'

And that was that.

Did you know that, to enable a taxi to spin around in tight spaces and perform U-turns in traffic, the cab is able to complete a 360° turn within a 25-foot diameter turning circle?

THE LONG ROAD TO ARDEN

My friend George McAteer picked up a hire one day in the Milton area of North Glasgow. The chap asked for a fixed price to Arden, deep in the South Side.

It was about nine miles and he was happy wih George's quote of £8. It was a fair price at the time.

The lad paid the fare before leaving Milton but when he arrived in Arden complained bitterly about the route George had taken him. George pointed out that, within reason, it couldn't matter which way he'd gone as the fare had been paid up front.

The guy was convinced he'd been ripped off and left the cab an unhappy chappie.

Can we never win?

THE BARE MINIMUM

The minimum charge for hiring a Glasgow taxi (in June 2003) is £1.80. This is the starting price and it covers a distance of up to 935 yards.

It's not uncommon for a driver to wait fifteen or twenty minutes on a taxi rank only to be approached by a customer wanting to go only a few hundred yards. This doesn't make for a happy driver, especially if the journey's unnecessary, for example just because a young lad can't be bothered to walk (and 'That's what taxis are there for.')

After a long wait on the taxi rank, a very short, unnecessary journey for the princely sum of £1.80 (and no gratuity to relieve the sting) is deeply insulting. It's even worse when the passenger is obviously being paid a lot more money than the driver earns.

To rub salt into the wound, after handing over exactly £1.80 some customers demand a receipt for this vast out-of-pocket expense. They'd not personally be any worse off if they were to add 50p for the driver – a receipt for £2.30 would make everybody happy. Thinking only of number one, however, what they'll do instead is pay £1.80 and then have the gall to ask the driver for an inflated receipt, say for £4 so that they can make a profit of £2.20 – which is more than the poor taxi driver got for his efforts.

At this point, when I'm asked to write out the inflated receipt that's worth £2.20 to our selfish little beggar, I add three words to the piece of paper that's going to be handed in to his accounts department: *Tight-fisted bastard!*

Sorry, but I have to remain sane and I find this helps – a little.

Sometimes they look at their receipts before leaving the cab but they always thank me. Up until now no one's ever complained. Just maybe the penny drops ...

A TAXI DRIVER'S MOAN

Having received a call to pick up at one of Glasgow's most prestigious City Centre hotels, I happily pulled away from the taxi rank where I'd just spent a long twenty minutes twiddling my thumbs.

On meeting the well-dressed gent and the blonde woman he was escorting, I was deflated to be told they weren't going far, it would only be a very short journey within the City Centre to a fine restaurant where they'd be shelling out fifty quid a head plus more for wine for the privilege of dining in style.

Even the smallest of fares is a welcome pick-up for a driver when he is 'on the run', but coming from a rank you need something a bit better. The fare I'd be receiving for this long-distance journey would be around £2.20. The fact that they were leaving an upmarket hotel for a swanky restaurant gave me hope that they'd subsidise my meagre fare. It looked like the gentleman was out to impress his lady friend and the paltry sum of £2.20 for such a personal and friendly service as I was preparing to give them would surely strike him as a mere pittance.

As they entered the vehicle I endeavoured to make my customers feel welcome and hid my inner demons that were bursting to demand how he had the audacity to summon a cab only to insult the driver with a journey of this trifling distance. It was more 'abuse of a taxi' than 'use of a taxi'.

'Busy tonight, driver?' my customer asked.

'It's really quiet tonight, sir, and I've spent the last twenty minutes sitting on the rank waiting for a call,' I said despondently.

We set off and almost immediately came to a halt in a queue of traffic. Making a perfect U-turn in the line of traffic from the outside lane took the cab to within a fraction of an inch of striking the opposite kerb with its nearside tyre. I was proud of my professionalism as I completed the 360° turn and swung left down a side lane to find a short cut out of the traffic.

Surprise was written all over the faces of my two passengers as I made my way slowly along the lane, exaggeratedly avoiding pot-holes as a professional driver does who deserves a little more than the bare fare for cleverly saving time by choosing a detour they hadn't known existed.

Surely they would appreciate this gallant attempt at customer care which rewarded my passengers with a smooth ride and a few minutes of quiet companionship. We duly arrived at the romantic restaurant. I thanked them and politely wished them a pleasant evening.

The meter showed the fare as just £2. I didn't announce it as it was clear for all to see.

'How much do I owe you, driver?' the gentleman enquired from the rear.

'It's only £2, sir,' I said, hoping he'd pick up on the 'only'.

Stretching out my hand, I felt two one-pound coins drop into my palm. No third coin.

I tried to make eye contact with my stingy passenger to communicate my opinion of his appreciation of services rendered. Having anticipated my response, he was already heading for the door with his lady for a good night out.

I felt abused and insulted. At times like that I feel this is the worst-paid job imaginable ... £2 in 30 minutes, less running expenses – before again falling heir to the last position on the rank for half an hour of kicking my heels. So £2 for a whole hour ...

My well-heeled customer may have managed to impress his lady but he certainly didn't impress me!

MY LONGEST TAXI JOURNEY

As soon as the idea came into my mind about writing this book, I started worrying about how to get it published. If I knew absolutely nothing about writing, I knew even less about publishing.

Billy Connolly's name immediately came to mind. If I could write a decent enough book about Glasgow's taxis and citizens, surely I could approach him on the grounds that we were both born in Anderston? He'd read it with admiration and point me in the direction of a publisher.

A little picture of him, in the bottom right-hand corner of the front cover, making a gesture of approval might springboard sales along nicely. Satisfied with that thought, I set about writing.

Two and a half years later I still had the same game plan. The time had come to approach my unsuspecting judge.

Billy has homes in the USA and Australia as well as Scotland, so I needed to consult the newspapers to find out which address to write to. I duly sent him a copy of my manuscript by Recorded Delivery. This set my mind at rest – I'd completed my task.

Weeks passed and I patiently awaited news ... from a publisher, an agent, anyone to whom Billy had delegated this trivial matter. What I didn't dare to hope for was a cold call from the Big Yin himself.

Nothing happened.

So what should I do? My faith in my plan made me doubt the safe delivery of my package.

After a debate with Irene, my wife, I convinced myself a small window of opportunity still existed – I could personally hand over another copy as Billy was in residence at his Highland retreat. The likes of Sean Connery, Dame Judi Dench and Michael Parkinson were likely to be adorning the place, transported by Rolls-Royce or Mercedes or Jaguar, but none would arrive in such salubrious splendour as I would in my Glasgow taxi.

I set out on my journey on Sunday August 24th 2003 at 2.30pm after a good sleep following my Saturday night shift. The journey started well – motorway up to the A9 at Dunkeld, then the A923 for the steep climb up to Blairgowrie and (watching the temperature gauge soar towards the red) the summit of the Glenshee ski slope. Catching a breather on the downward slope, I watched anxiously as the gauge returned to normal before I started the final climb towards Strathdon.

This section reminded me of the Eaglesham Moors road where I'd come across the dead sheep in the middle of the road. No sooner had this thought struck me than I found myself flying past a dead pheasant on the white line in the middle of the road. This was a good omen. I about-turned, retrieved the pheasant and carefully stored it in the boot of the taxi. It would make a good gift for Billy. I was starting to get nervous about reaching my destination.

One stop to ask directions, then I had arrived.

The smiling faces of security personnel in full highland dress greeted me as I came to a halt at the gate. They were very pleasant and asked if I'd driven all the way from Glasgow. The sight of a Glasgow taxi had indeed made its mark. Never had they seen a cab as far north as this – and just to deliver one little parcel. They were impressed.

Enquiries to the office via their security headsets told me exactly what I'd expected to hear. The principal was entertaining guests and couldn't be disturbed – but they'd be only too pleased to take my package and make sure Mr Connolly got it later. At least I was pleased they'd taken the time to make me feel at ease rather than just brushing me off.

Me proudly displaying the Big Yin's pheasant

Feeling nervous and outnumbered in strange territory, I slipped a badly scribbled note inside my book cover asking to be contacted if anything could be done to help me get it published. Thanking the security guards for their patience, I returned to the cab for the long journey home. The milometer told me that it was 167 miles from my home to Billy's gate.

Whether I'd achieved anything with this audacious journey remained to be seen. The return journey would make it a 334-mile round trip. A journey of that distance on a motorway would take about five hours, but this was a hard climb from the start to the midway point, with twists and turns all the way. The return leg would start off well, with its downward slalom, but soon a hard journey will start to take its toll on a 51-year-old driver. My 4-year-old TX1 cab did better than I did and in my opinion its performance compared favourably with that of the four-wheel-drive vehicles that frequent the area.

Driving through the tranquil Scottish Highlands I began to laugh at myself for not handing over the pheasant to the security men to pass on to the principal himself. It remained locked in the boot until I posed for this photograph two days later.

I eventually got back home at 10.30pm: total journey time 8 hours. Just enough time to dump my faithful cab and head for the pub for a large one.

I considered my journey. It was successful in that I'd made contact with my chosen judge. Also, for the first time, I'd had the opportunity to test the TX1 in unfamiliar territory and judge how it handled when climbing and turning. Without being too biased towards the machine I earn a living from, I consider its performance superb. And fuel consumption was 12p per mile, not bad for that type of terrain.

As this book's going to print, I've been unsuccessful contacting Billy himself. His office in London returned my book with a small note wishing me luck.

Did you know that often, when a driver pulls up outside a pub after being flagged down, he's asked to take more passengers than he's legally permitted to carry? The request is usually along these lines: 'You'll git a guid bung, driver, if ye take an extra wan.' Have you ever made this request yourself?

The Glasgow Taxi Trade

THE DEVELOPING VEHICLE

The Beardmore

Introduced in 1919 by Beardmore Motors Ltd (a subsidiary of the Beardmore steel and shipbuilding conglomerate) at their Inderwood works in Paisley, the Beadrmore taxi's slogan was, 'For comfort and speed it's all you need.' At a cost of £690, it came complete with electric lighting and automatic starter.

The Beardmore in the Glasgow Transport Museum: 'This "Hyper" Mk III London Taxi Cab is one of two known survivors. Beardmore built taxis to this design at their Paisley and Anniesland works from May 1929 to 1933. It was popular with cabbies as it was easier to drive than earlier taxis. The 1954cc four-cylinder, side valve, water-cooled monobloc engine produced 12.8hp (RAC rating).'

In 1929 Beardmore introduced the Hyper Mk III, with a four-cylinder 1954cc engine, improved steering and four wheel brakes. Produced until 1933, the Hyper was the backbone of Beardmore's production. However, as at many other Scottish factories facing the axe, production ceased in Scotland and was moved to new premises in Hendon in north-west London.

There followed the Paramount Mk IV, with the Mk V in 1936 and the Mk VI in 1937, each with improvements, until the outbreak of war halted production in 1939.

The Beardmore Mk VII

It was not until 1954 that Beardmore produced the Mk VII, fitted with a 1508cc Ford Consul engine and gearbox, and then with a Perkins Four 99 diesel engine in

1958. This advanced machine, with an aluminium and glass fibre body made by Windovers of Hendon, was very popular with drivers. About 650 were built before production ceased in 1967.

The Mk VIII never reached the production line but became the new Mk VIII concept of MCW (Metropolitan Cammell Weymann) and was the basis of the new Metrocab. Beardmore closed in 1969.

Beardmore interior

134

The FX3

The first taxi I remember was my father's Austin FX3. I always thought it a beautiful vehicle, with a long straight bonnet that lifted up from both sides of the cab, and long curved front wings that ran down to the running boards, sweeping along the vehicle to meet the rear wings. The bulbous painted headlamps on either side of the chrome fluted grill also impressed me.

Chrome bumpers and overriders front and rear were standard, and chrome hubcaps and wheel-trims. The glossy black paintwork lavishly reflected the chrome in the bodywork. A stainless steel luggage compartment encased a large toolbox. Inside the cab was a rich smell of real leather upholstery – a wonderful, unique smell.

Positioning myself behind the steering wheel at a tender age enthralled me. The steering wheel had chrome supports meeting in the centre, at the button horn, in which was also encased an inch-long switch to operate the semaphore indicators on the early model – or roof indicators on later FX3 designs.

Cab and passenger heaters were non-existent. More seriously, the Girling braking system left much to be desired – braking on Glasgow's wet cobbles was almost impossible.

The FX3 was introduced in 1948 with a standard 2199cc petrol engine. It was not until 1954 that the popular 2.2-litre diesel engine was fitted. Sales of diesel vehicles soon outstripped petrol – by 1955 nine diesel cabs were sold for every petrol version.

The dealership responsible for sales and distribution was the well-known Mann & Overton of London, who launched the vehicle from their Wandsworth Bridge Road premises at a total cost of £936 1s 8d.

Carbodies, the Coventry coachbuilders, manufactured the bodies until the FX3 ceased production in 1958.

The FX4

I first caught sight of the new FX4 in 1959 at the Carlaw Cars showroom in Finneston Street. My first impression was that it looked like a Rolls-Royce. The new design was striking. Most of its features had been taken from its predecessor, but they'd been improved in almost every way.

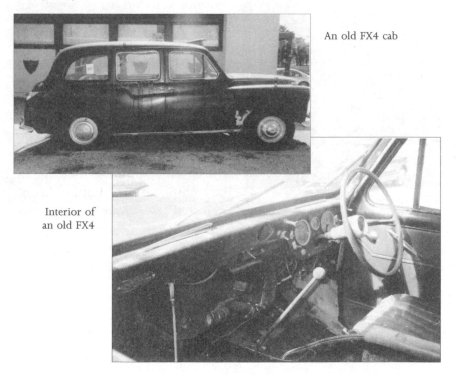

An old FX4 cab

Interior of an old FX4

A fourth door for the luggage compartment was the most obvious design change. The curves between the front wings and bonnet were retained but a squarer grill and flatter front gave the FX4 a more modern look. Comfort was improved by a passenger compartment heater and interior lighting, both of which could be controlled by the customer.

Driver comfort was also considered, the driver's cabin being enclosed for the first time and a heater fitted. A redesigned dashboard added to the vehicle's modern look. The Austin badge and motif were proudly displayed on the front grill and bonnet, and a single fog lamp came as standard.

An Austin 2.2-litre diesel engine was fitted, although a petrol version was also available. All vehicles had an automatic gearbox, with no option of a manual version when the vehicle was first introduced. The Borg Warner automatic gearbox, popular in London, proved a disaster on the streets of Glasgow where the many hills were so punishing that the life of the gearbox was in many cases only six months.

In its lifetime the FX4 underwent many design and mechanical changes. The two 6-volt batteries were replaced by a single 12-volt, rooftop indicators were incorporated in the rear wings, the old dynamo was replaced by an alternator, improved heaters were a huge success, and in 1971 a 2.5-litre diesel engine boosted performance. This brought the cost of an FX4 up to £1,612.

An old advertisement for an FX4

The FX4 was with us all the way from 1959 to 1989, its various improvements marked by changing model numbers, and eventually culminating in the Fairway. Production of the Fairway started in 1989, but not before a huge change in the industry.

LTI, London Taxi International — originally Carbodies (coachbuilders of the FX3 and FX4), whose parent

137

company Manganese Bronze had bought out Mann & Overton (who spearheaded sales and distribution) – had taken over production of the FX4 from British Leyland in 1987. LTI manufactured the old FX4 for another two years before introducing the most impressive and most popular model in the range, the Fairway.

The Fairway

The Fairway kept the look of the old FX4 but it was a total transformation of the original version which had come out thirty years before. There was a whole list of improvements including a powerful 2.7-litre Nissan diesel engine, a 5-speed manual gearbox, disc brakes, power steering, upgraded suspension, an intercom system between driver and passenger, greatly improved safety screens, central locking, a re-designed interior, wheelchair accessibility, electric windows, an electronic internal taximeter, an adjustable driver's seat with lumbar support and split rear passenger seats which could lift up to make more floor space available for wheelchair users (enabling them to turn and face their fellow travellers).

LTI ceased production of the Fairway in 1997. So the FX4, which had first appeared in 1959 and ended life as the Fairway, had lasted for a staggering 38 years. In the biggest gamble in their history, LTI then began manufacturing the Fairway's long-awaited replacement, the TX1.

The Metrocab

The first purpose-built wheelchair-accessible taxi to operate in Glasgow was the Metrocab, introduced in 1986. Built by Metropolitan Cammell Weymann of Birmingham, it was descended from two prototypes built as far back as 1970, but was more directly based on the design for the extinct Beardmore Mk VIII project acquired in 1978.

With its fibreglass body, larger passenger compartment and improved driver visibility, it soon became popular. It was fitted with a 2.5-litre Ford Transit diesel engine and gearbox.

The Reliant Motor Group took over the production of the Metrocab and opened a new assembly plant in Tamworth in 1990, where at its peak they were producing eight vehicles a week. In January 2004, however, Metrocab went into administration.

The TX1

Inheriting all the popular features of the well-proven Fairway, the outwardly transformed TX1 was an immediate success. Its design took into account the changing cab trade and in particular the new Disability Act. Because of its extra height it soon became known as the Noddy car.

The TX1 cab

It was, however, a very serious design, created to help customers with difficulties make their trips that little bit more easily. The extra height, particularly the extra height of the door aperture, greatly improved access for wheelchair-users who could now be pushed up a ramp into the cab without even having to bend their heads.

Steel ramps for wheelchair access, standard on the first TX1s, have been replaced by an integral ramp pulled out from the passenger compartment floor. This greatly reduces the time a wheelchair passenger has to spend at the roadside as it is no longer necessary for the driver to have to take the ramps from the boot and fit them.

The TX1 with its new integral ramp for wheelchair access

Other improvements are brightly coloured grab-handles and foot-lights at the entrance, which help the partially sighted gain safe access. A laptop power point is of course a must for business users. Vanity mirrors have also been installed for passenger convenience and the rear seat armrest converts into a baby seat. Such attention to detail makes the TX1 a real winner.

Did you know that, when the new TX1 was introduced in 1997, with it came a revolutionary new intercom system which amplified voice volume, allowing a conversation to take place between passenger and driver? Most people are pleasantly surprised to hear their voices boom into the driver's compartment, overcoming the sound wall that the partition between front and rear compartments creates. It may surprise many, including the drivers of these vehicles, that as far back as 1929 a Bourovox communication system was installed in some vehicles allowing dialog through a microphone.

The Eurotaxi

It was in 1999 that the Eurotaxi first plied for hire on the streets of Glasgow.

Supplied by the Peugeot dealership Cab Direct in Possilpark, this 2-litre van conversion soon proved a success, being much cheaper than custom-built vehicles. At £20,000 there was a saving of £8,000 or £9,000 on a TX1 or Metrocab respectively. Fuel consumption was also remarkably good at 35 mpg. Extra pulling power was available by the end of 2001 when the output of the 1997cc Peugeot engine was increased to 110bhp. But drawbacks remain in the form of sliding doors to the passenger compartment and the poor turning circle.

The Euro 7 model can carry seven passengers comfortably and still have room for their luggage in the rear. Glasgow City Council have licensed the vehicle to carry six passengers.

Did you know that at the 1920 Olympia Motorcycle Show a number of side-car taxis were exhibited by well-known motor-cycle makers such as Campion, Rex, BSA and Excelsior? The Campion seated two passengers side by side, while the Rex had staggered seating. The first of these new taxis went into service in Glasgow in December 1920, charging fares 33% lower than ordinary taxis.

DOOR DESIGN

It was only when I started to put pen to paper that I fully realised how far taxi door design has come over the years.

The FX3 had only three doors, as its name indicates. Although a purpose-built taxi, it didn't even have a partition between driver and luggage compartment, so the driver was open to the elements. On a nice summer's day he wouldn't need air conditioning, but in winter, Scottish weather being unforgiving, many almost froze to death. Some sort of headgear, a scarf and gloves were necessary. A luggage compartment door was sorely missed. Towards the end of FX3 manufacture a partition was introduced between driver and luggage compartment so that he was at least sheltered from the weather.

The FX4 had a dynamic new shape and the much-needed near-side front door for the luggage compartment. This solved the problem of a driver suffering from exposure and provided a secure environment for him to work in. Customers' luggage was also safe now – many a suitcase had been thrown from a quickly cornering FX3, and clothing strewn across the road. The new lockable front door also of course improved the security of the vehicle.

Unfortunately, however, the rear passenger doors could not be locked so the back of the cab was at the mercy of the midnight public. It wasn't long before every tramp in town knew where to get a free bed for the night, on luxurious leather, what's more, with a leather armrest pillow — much nicer than a bench or bus shelter! No draughts, no booking fee, and an early wake-up call guaranteed.

Every day-shift driver had to check the back for 'sleepers' before starting work. A solution to this problem had to be forthcoming, and it was. The problem-solving skills of the taxi trade have always impressed me. We'll always find solutions. Some brilliant, some not so wonderful. The solution in this case was two 6-inch nails.

Holes were drilled and the nails pushed through the door pillars into the rear doors. Virtually impregnable!

This also went a long way to solving the problem of the 'runner'. If a driver suspected he had a runner in the back, he'd open his own door and insert the nail to secure the passenger door behind him. This could be done without raising suspicion if he made it look as if his door hadn't closed properly. The other passenger door was more difficult to secure, but it had to be done. It required the opening of the luggage door, so the driver had to get out and approach from the pavement side. If he could achieve this then the passenger had no means of escape, he'd either have to pay the fare or spend the night in one of Her Majesty's hotels. Days were becoming more difficult for the runner.

The biggest problem with doors now was not one of security but one of safety. The passenger doors opened in the opposite direction to the front doors, and into oncoming traffic, against the airflow. They were known as suicide doors. If a door was opened when the cab was moving, the wind would catch it and throw it open with tremendous force, breaking the retaining strap and crashing it into the rear wing. The result was a smashed door, a buckled rear wing and a damaged door pillar. At present values the repair would cost £1,000.

Because the rear doors could not be locked (except by being nailed) these accidents were often caused by doors being opened before the cab actually stopped because passengers wished to make a quick exit. The problem was compounded by the fact that at that time lampposts on pavements were always positioned at the very edge of the kerb, close to the road. There was always an accident waiting to happen.

I wish I had a shilling for every time a passenger said to me, as I was travelling at 30 mph, 'Just stop here driver – right at this lamp-post!'

I always tried to comply but, with experience and the grace of God, managed to avoid hitting lampposts. Not every cabbie was so lucky. As the delinquent passenger hastily paid the fare, made his excuses and scuttled off, the driver would be left left with a big headache and massive repair bill.

Not every passenger managed to strike a pole. Sometimes a lady friend was awaiting his arrival. Eager to get out, he'd luckily miss the pole but open the door just as she was coming to welcome him. *Splat!* I leave the scene to your imagination.

Over the years doors became more driver- and passenger-friendly. The TX1 and Metrocab were designed with passenger doors opening towards the back, as in private vehicles. This would have been no simple task as they had to open to ninety degrees to allow even heavy and wide electric wheelchairs to enter without restriction. The door retaining strap was redesigned, becoming detachable for wheelchair entry.

The new doors not only prevent exiting when the cab is in motion, they also bleep when left open and when the vehicle stops. A continuous piercing buzz sounds when the door is not closed properly and warning lights on the dashboard show the driver the door's position. The windows in the doors open electrically – much easier for the customer – but can be overridden by the driver. State of the art or what?

I'll finish this section with the first and last thing a customer has contact with on entering and leaving the cab: the door handle. In early vehicles, and until recently, the door handles were made to last and be secure, but this did not make them passenger friendly. They were difficult to open, especially for the elderly and arthritic.

For years passengers struggled with the handles and many simply failed. For years I'd have to leave my seat and go round to help. For these people I had all the time in the world, I didn't resent the effort. It wasn't their fault. It was my job. Members of the public often complained if a driver didn't get out to open the door and I'm sure in many cases the complaints were justified.

But some who struggled, or appeared to struggle, managed to master the handle just as you'd made the effort to come round and help. Some were seeking attention, others just found it amusing to get the driver out of his saddle. Some of these were well known to drivers. It was knowing what they knew that made some drivers refuse to help in many cases. Unfortunately for us the public didn't see it our way.

Sometimes I'd play games with myself and try to guess which passenger would need help opening the door and which wouldn't. A decent driver could guess pretty accurately.

When a customer was struggling and the driver knew it was an act, he'd wait until the customer actually looked at him for help. Then he'd lean over and switch the meter on. It was amazing how many doors then opened instantly.

As they always did of course when it was pouring cats and dogs.

Now that doors offer no challenge another laugh is over – but its all in the name of progress.

Did you know that?

LONDON PURPOSE BUILT TAXI GAINS THUMBS UP FROM WOMEN IN INDEPENDENT SURVEY

An independent survey recently undertaken by NOP has revealed that 86% of nearly 500 women interviewed feel safe in the familiar London style 'black cab' in Britain's capital.

The results of the survey have been announced at a time when the issue of safety in cabs is at an all time high following the recent announcement by the Metropolitan Police that one woman a week is raped in London alone after accepting a ride in an illegal mini cab.

A FASTER BLACK

Hailing a cab before the 1950s was a very basic procedure. You either put your hand up in the street or went to a taxi rank.

It was not until the 'fifties that technology started to change the taxi trade. A customer could now for the first time telephone for a taxi. This was no sophisticated system, just a simple telephone fixed about six feet up a telegraph pole at the front of the taxi rank. (It had to be high enough for children to be unable to reach it.)

Cab owners had by this time formed themselves into the Taxi Owners Association or TOA, whose job it was to enhance earning potential and protect the interests of members, and it was they who had introduced this service.

Soon there were telephones at most main taxi ranks, with the phone number of the rank painted in black on the yellow canopy over the telephone. Each canopy also bore the rhyme:

The service here is
  night and day,
Supplied to you by TOA.

Can you remember?
   The public now had a third way of hiring a cab. The first TOA car on the rank always took the call but if there were no TOA taxis then any cab driver could answer.

A Fast Black with personalised registration plate

It was not until the early 'sixties that the TOA opened an office in Lynedoch Street, Charing Cross and started to supply their members with the latest telecommunications wonder, *two-way radio*. This was a huge leap forward. Instead of a customer having to telephone a rank and take his chance as to availability he could now ring the office and get an immediate answer and know that the controller would despatch the nearest cab available. This driver-friendly system became known as 'the radio'.

Everyone could hear everything that was said over the air, so everyone got to know each other. Each car had its own ID and everyone was known by his call sign. When a controller despatched you on a job he'd usually end by acknowledging your name for all to hear.

Whenever a driver or 'mobile' got into the cab in the morning and switched on his radio, there was always a friendly voice to say 'Good morning' and acknowledge that he was starting his shift, or 'signing on' as it was known.

Because all work despatched over the air was heard by everyone, drivers got to know about regular passengers even before they picked them up. Regular work was 'clocked' by every driver and most of them remembered at what time of day a regular would be calling for a cab.

The radio room was introduced at the time when telephones were beginning to be installed in many family homes, though it would be several years before most households had them.

Friction arose between the TOA and some taxi owners. The owners could all clearly see the financial advantages of having two-way radio in their cabs and were unhappy to drive without it. The TOA, however, were unwilling to give everyone a radio. Their duty was to protect the interests of their members and they weren't sure that the business from telephone work could sustain the large number of taxi owners now demanding radios.

The inevitable happened: the introduction of a second radio system. The Taxi Cab Association or TCA was formed in my father's house at 445 St Vincent Street, Anderston and premises were found in a first floor flat in an Eglinton Street tenement on the South Side of the city. The aim of the TCA was to take on all the work in that area. They were soon a formidable opponent for the TOA.

They were nicknamed 'The South' – or 'White Flag', because of the white flag with distinctive red lettering displayed on the roofs of their vehicles. The TOA had not changed their colours since the days of the yellow and black taxi-rank telephone canopies.

A third radio system then sprang to life, covering mainly the East End of the city. This was the Glasgow Radio Taxi Association whose distinguishing ID was a red flag on the roof. Their premises were on London Road in Bridgeton, hence the nickname 'Bridgeton'.

Flags from the taxis

Years passed with all three systems operating successfully but it eventually became clear that three radio systems in the city were too many. Costs needed to be cut. Bridgeton and the TCA amalgamated, which increased the number of vehicles on the TCA system from 200 to 300. The TOA had 400.

The Glasgow Taxis railway bridge

148

Not everyone welcomed the loss of Bridgeton and a new third system arose in its wake. Identified by a pink flag on the roof, they inevitably became known as 'The Pinkies'. They in turn eventually had to concede that a third radio system was uneconomical.

They also amalgamated with the TCA, which changed its name to Glasgow Wide in a bid to attract work from all over the city, not just the South and East.

In 1997 the big two, TOA and Glasgow Wide, held several meetings to seek common ground for a merger. Unsuccessful at first, after many changes on both sides the amalgamation went ahead. Both names were manipulated into their new title, The Glasgow Wide Taxi Owners Association. This merger created the biggest taxi firm in the country, now controlling 900 cabs. In the interests of simplicity the company name has become

The old TOA had previously upgraded from two-way radio to the computerised GANDAF despatch system and now the old Glasgow Wide cabs had to follow suit to take advantage of the improved technology with its extensive computer banks. Voice despatch for a system as large as this was not an option.

The Raywood Global Positioning Satellite System has today replaced GANDAF at a cost of £1m (a sizeable investment!) in the drive for a faster, more efficient service. The signal leaves the office in Glasgow, zooms out into space to a satellite, and is bounced straight back to the cab nearest the pick-up. In a nanosecond!

The driver can read every detail of a customer's requirements on a small screen above the dashboard.

The computer display screen above the steering wheel of a TX1

Name of customer
Address of pick-up
Job reference number
Destination

including any special requirements:

Pick up at back door
Passenger in wheelchair, please assist
Dog to accompany him.

The driver is also informed whether the customer is paying by cash, card or credit account. Two map references are given for pick-up and destination – this saves valuable time if either is obscure. Every road in a 30-mile radius of Glasgow is programmed into the computer, so even if your pick-up's in Dumbarton you'll get a grid reference to guide you right to the spot.

The most recent radio room development is Interactive Voice Response (we call it Ivor), by which a customer can order a taxi without going through the switchboard, simply by phoning 429-7070, following instructions and pressing the right button. Hey presto! A cab appears as if by magic.

The new Glasgow Taxis advertising the phone number

Technology has come a long way in the last forty years – but the customer still gets a Fast Black.

THE DESIGNER TAXI

In the 'sixties new vehicles rolling off the assembly line were all identical. They had no extras. They were standard black FX4s – only in London was a variance in colour permitted.

Once purchased, and before it could legally ply for hire on the streets of Glasgow, a cab had to have its owner's name and licence number painted onto the passenger doors. The only way of doing this then was by sign-writing, which involved the skilful painting of each individual character. This gave the new cab owner the chance of customising his vehicle at the same time.

The most popular embellishment was a mid-way gold line right round the whole cab. As this sort of decoration became more popular, bolder designs were introduced. Some started with a scroll

at the front grill, ran down both sides and finished with a similar scroll on the rear boot door. Some designs encircled the number plate and front grill.

Even today it's popular to have cabs fully sign-written, with family names on the rear. Many drivers will choose a colour for the decorative line that associates them with a particular football club.

Green line	=	Celtic
Blue line	=	Rangers
Red and Yellow	=	Neutral
		– or possibly Partick Thistle.

There were also other ways of making your cab stand out. You could fit spot or fog lights or have personalised markings or badges on the front grill. Distinctive wheeltrims could be fitted. If you were lucky enough to have all of these everyone would know your cab before it even turned the corner.

Tommy Crombie was sign-writer for the Glasgow cabs in the 'sixties to the 'eighties and did almost every cab that came onto the city streets. Like many associated with the cab trade, he was a character. He had a joke for every panel he painted.

Did you know that the first taxi licence plate Glasgow City Council issued was white in colour and replaced the old half-moon device that was painted onto the rear boot of the vehicle? The current black licence plate also displays the licence number of the cab on the boot door, and a similar plate is displayed on the front grill.

The old half-moon and the current-day licence plates

THE DIFFERENCE BETWEEN A REAL TAXI AND PRIVATE HIRE

The difference between a private hire car and a real taxi is sometimes difficult for the public to grasp. Different rules apply in different parts of the UK but what I can tell you about is the situation in Glasgow.

Many think that the private hire trade here is part of the taxi trade but it is completely separate. Okay, the difference isn't as clear as the difference between a butcher's shop and an ice cream parlour but it's still fundamental.

Both trades transport passengers from A to B, but there are important differences. Glasgow City Council stipulate clearly which vehicles are allowed to ply for hire as taxis. They have to comply with strict specifications to safeguard the public, in particular the disabled. In other words they have to be *purpose-built vehicles*. The most popular Glasgow taxi is the TXI or II, the most recent model of the old London taxi, which costs £30,000.

Add to this the cost of buying a taxi business, add finance and legal charges, and the new owner can be committing himself to an investment of around £60,000, a sizable sum. To repay this outlay he'll need to keep the cab working 24/7. But he'll give the public the very best professional service. He's not in the trade for a fast buck, he's made a commitment for years to come. In return he expects to make a decent living wage from his investment, and a profit from the sale of the business when he retires.

The private hire business is far less regulated. There is no restriction on the number of private-hire licences issued and almost anyone can get into the business, with a minimum of experience and outlay. All he'll need is a four-door vehicle of some sort (anything from a brand new Skoda to an old Ford Escort from the car market), a £250 licence from Glasgow City Council, £40 for a vehicle inspection test at the Council garages, proof that his first payment towards insurance cover has been made and to join one of the many private hire systems. He does not need to satisfy the Council that he has a thorough knowledge of Glasgow streets by sitting a topographical test, nor is he obliged to make provision for wheelchair users.

Seeing customers picked up by private hire cars while real taxis sit and wait for work naturally chokes us real cabbies. Please don't just use us for that trip to the station with extra luggage! The Glasgow taxi trade has served its people well over the years and can offer a better, faster service than ever before. With the exception of Aberdeen, our cabs are the cheapest city taxis in Scotland.

Did you know that due to the volume of traffic in London and the large number of one-driver cabs, the average Glasgow taxi does many more miles in a year that its London counterpart?

THE SELF-EMPLOYED TAXI DRIVER

The self-employed taxi driver enjoys many advantages, especially when it comes to the freedom to work as he pleases.

No boss breathing down his neck, scrutinising his working practices. No more reprimands from the powers that be upstairs about time-keeping and days off. If he wants to follow his football team, that's fine. Work can be rearranged. No more clocking in and clocking out. For the first time ever the clock isn't his enemy. Holidays can be taken when he wants them. No worries about getting away that day or two earlier, and never mind the airport delay coming back, no humble pie to be eaten because he didn't make it in on Monday morning. He just works an extra couple of extra hours here and there and he's fine.

You need to understand the difference between a driver, an owner-driver and an operator. A driver and owner-driver do the same job but the driver rents the cab from an owner-driver or operator at a fixed rate (depending on hours worked). It's the owner or operator's responsibility to finance and maintain the vehicle.

Every driver can choose whether to work day shift or night shift, or have the vehicle at his disposal 24/7. This last is known as a single shift and allows the driver to pick and choose his hours and work the most lucrative hours at weekend peak periods. A single-shifted driver has to bear the whole cost of running the vehicle, though of course wear and tear on a single-shifted cab is less than on a double-shifted one.

The amount paid by a driver to hire a taxi, the 'weigh-in', varies from owner to owner and also reflects the age of the cab. A radio cab less than three years old would probably command a day-shift weigh-in of £185 and a night-shift weigh-in of £200.

A cab less than five years old would normally not be single-shifted as the weigh-in would need to include hire-purchase costs in the region of £130 a week, which would make it too expensive for one driver. It is normally the older vehicles that are down-graded from double- to single-shifted drivers.

A driver will be able to choose whether to have a radio or work the streets. The weigh-in for a single-shifted radio cab would be about £245 a week, and about £60 less for a non-radio cab.

Being in the self-employed cab trade is not like working for a boss, where forty hours a week are worked for a regular wage. As soon as the self-employed driver sits behind the wheel of the cab, he owes the cab owner a weigh-in. He starts his working week owing (if he's a single-shifted driver) £245 for the cab and another £45 for diesel. And let's not forget the cost of a self-employed National Insurance stamp – that will bring his overheads up to about £300. Only after he's paid that off will he start to earn money for himself. It starts to look like a huge price to pay for the privilege of having no boss.

Somewhere in the middle of the week – or towards the end if he's had time off – our single-shifted driver will break even and start earning for himself. It's usually at weekends that vehicles manage to acquire mechanical or electrical problems, but let's be optimistic and assume the cab stays in good health, and the driver too, and that he sees the week out.

Our driver, after working nights at the weekend, having the honour of serving the Glasgow public to the best of his ability, treating obnoxious drunks, fare-dodgers, schizophrenics, story-tellers and all the erratic drivers out there with equal respect and coping with traffic jams, unsequenced traffic lights, speed cameras and the ever-increasing number of senseless speed bumps that knock hell out of his back, will hopefully finish his working week with a respectable financial reward.

So you think we taxi drivers have it all our own way? If you're sitting comfortably in a salaried office job, with an occupational pension scheme, sickness benefits, holiday pay and all those little perks you don't really count, just think again. The self-employed cab driver has none of these benefits. Imagine the delight on the face of a hire to Easterhouse when he's told the fare is £5 plus 50p for the driver's holiday and sickness pay and another 50p to top up his pension fund.

When our driver's financial year ends and all his weekly takings are tallied up, it's the turn of the Inland Revenue to aim – and they never miss. The self-employed driver is a soft target. The settlement figure they arrive at is always in their favour but most drivers simply agree to it. They don't have the stomach to take on such a powerful body, they're suffering from financial diarrhoea.

All this fun and no promotion at the end of it.

To be honest, I've surprised myself by writing up so many reasons not to be a self-employed cab driver. I wonder why I've stuck it for so long? So very long!

Did you know that there are 1,428 licensed taxis in Glasgow? Each cab is inspected once a year ('the big one') and has an interim routine test after six months, just to make sure everything's in good condition. Before each examination the vehicle must be steam cleaned underneath and in the engine compartment. If it fails the test it must be re-presented within seven days. If a serious fault is found the testing station will remove the licensing plates as the vehicle will have been deemed unsafe to work. It will not be allowed to operate as a taxi until the necessary repairs have been carried out.

TAXI DRIVER TO TAXI OWNER

The time will duly come when a driver decides to go for it and buy his own taxi business.

He'll do the rounds of the banks seeking finance and be told to produce accounts for the past financial year. When he's done this to their satisfaction he'll be asked for a projection for the next financial year as an owner driver. If this also satisfies the banking fraternity, he is eventually given approval to proceed.

To keep expenses to a minimum he will need to choose an older vehicle (that will nevertheless remain roadworthy) so that payments remain within the realms of possibility while he finds his feet.

He's now an owner-driver.

To maximise his earning potential he'll join the city radio system so that, in addition to picking up fares on the street, he can pick up radio calls. This will probably be an expense he'd not yet taken into account. Glasgow Taxis recognises this and offers new members a deal by which they can spread the cost of the joining fee.

From day one the new owner will have been required to invest around £30,000 in his new business venture.

He'll go home and tell the neighbours there'll be a change of taxi at his door – he'll no longer be driving for a boss! No common worker him. He's now the architect of his own finances, an entre-preneur! His neighbours will be impressed and not realise the magnitude of the financial commitment he has had to make. He must be doing very nicely to afford his own cab.

This is the perception at the end of Stage 1.

Stage 2. After tying his shoelaces to the pedals for eighteen months the new taxi owner will face a dilemma. His cab is due for its annual mechanical and body test, 'the inspection'. This is carried out by Glasgow City Council Garages and is very stringent. Every mechan-ical aspect is checked, suspension, steering, brakes, you name it. And the bodywork – whether the paintwork's up to scratch. It's bound to be an expensive time. He'll have to correct all listed faults; need-less or not, all repairs must be carried out.

Often the owner is required to repaint parts of the cab; in extreme cases a full respray is called for. Apart from the cost, this results in down-time. The vehicle may be off the road for a week for paint-work, perhaps another two or three days for mechanical work and steam cleaning of the underside and engine compartment.

The dilemma is whether it is likely to be cheaper for him to buy a new vehicle. The decision is usually yes. This will reduce the prob-lems to one of cashflow only. No inspection, no down-time, no repair bills.

John Paton & Son, the London Taxi International dealership in Glasgow

Taking delivery of his brand new vehicle and the bill, he will add on the unpaid balance of his original investment and find his total borrowings now exceed £50,000.

The neighbours will see it differently. A new cab outside his front door will prove he's making a fortune. After only eighteen months! He's making so much money he's not only bought himself a business but a brand new cab to go with it!

After sorting out teething troubles with the new cab and paying for his radio equipment to be transferred he's back on the road. He's quite content with his new little empire. All he needs is to bring in the money to pay for it all.

Stage 3. The night shift is always more lucrative than the day, and there are not nearly as many traffic problems at night. Realising this, and having the need to maximise his earnings, he'll change his routine to 8pm to 6am. Night shift equals cash in, bills out. Problem solved.

His neighbours see it another way. They'll get up in the morning and see the new taxi sitting outside doing nothing. At lunchtime it will still be there. When they get home for tea it's obvious it hasn't been anywhere at all. Clearly there's so much money in the business the owner doesn't have to work. After tea they close the curtains and count their own sorrows.

That's when the taxi leaps into life and hits the street, giving our great city the service it deserves. Ten hours later our weary night-shift driver cuts off the engine and falls into bed.

His friendly neighbour opens the curtains and confirms his opinion. *Never works, that guy — no need to...*

It'll take him five years to pay for the licence. Another two or three before he owns his vehicle. Something like that.

Did you know that CCTV cameras are now being installed in taxicabs? You can't get away from Big Brother. Throughout the country pilot schemes are being evaluated. A spokesman for The National Taxi Association said, 'This is something which is beginning to happen nationwide. The idea is for driver safety and passenger safety to be improved. If it does not prevent incidents, it might help to seal a conviction.'

TAXI INSURANCE

Now this must be the most boring subject I know. The only people interested in insurance are those who work in the business.

The only time I had a laugh in an insurance office was when the agent told me about a claim form he'd just received from a lady customer. She stated that she'd been travelling along a country road in dreadful weather conditions. Driving wind and snow made visibility very poor. Suddenly she saw a tree had blown down in front of her and lay stretched across the road. She swerved to avoid the tree — and hit the stump.

I put cab insurance in the necessary evil bracket. Necessary because of course you have to cover the vehicle and passengers for any eventuality. Evil because it's just another money pit. You get charged every year to cover the same item you paid for last year. Make a claim and — *whack!* — up goes the premium. Keeping premiums managable means guarding your no-claims bonus, not an easy task, and quite impossible if you're hit by an uninsured driver.

I remember the message I once saw on a notice board outside a church in Anderston: 'Oh, the relief of losing my No-Claims Bonus!'

Cab insurance, including passenger liability cover, is a major cost for a taxi operator. Today's compensation culture and the number of law firms offering 'no win, no fee' lawsuits in personal injury cases has sent shockwaves through the insurance industry and sent premiums through the roof. The annual cost of cab insurance without a no-claims bonus is now something like £3,000. 'Insurance time' is one of the most costly periods for a cab operator.

Did you know that as crowds of revellers exit from late-night clubs at weekends, taxi ranks are soon besieged by hundreds of impatient customers? Sometimes the queue is so excessive people start walking homewards, hoping to pick up a cab on the way. They can't understand why empty taxis shoot past them. Some get quite aggressive towards the drivers, thinking that they're refusing to pick them up because they're expecting better fares going longer distances from the City Centre, or because they don't want to go in that particular direction.

Neither is true. It's just that we have to clear the City Centre taxi ranks. If all the cabs stopped and picked up before they reached them, the public queuing there would have one hell of a long wait.

Think about it. At that time of night there's probably no work for taxi drivers except in the City Centre, so many cabs are returning empty from outlying areas. It would actually suit them very well to pick up a fare before they reached a City Centre rank.

Trying to service the ranks efficiently and keep queues to a minimum won't satisfy everybody. If only all the public could see it from our side.

PEAK PERIODS

The morning rush. During school term time, when our little darlings are soaking up their education, the taxi trade is busiest during the working day. Between 8am and 9am demand for cabs is greatest, especially on Monday mornings. Workers running late scream for taxis, schoolchildren need picking up, office workers want to drop their children off at school and then get in to town for their own working day. This is the time telephones in the radio room go crazy with the demands of more desperate callers and irate customers who've been waiting thirty minutes.

Extreme efforts are made by telephonists, control staff and drivers to minimise delay and it's only the minority of customers that experience any serious problems. But there are some, inevitably, and I can see no solution.

Glasgow is a big city, and all big cities have big congestion problems. The public are not always prepared to understand that, as well as being the time of day when demand is greatest, 8am-9am is also the time when traffic jams reach crisis levels. The journey time from the outskirts to the City Centre can double at this time. The West End is likely to be totally gridlocked.

This sort of traffic mayhem is what both customers and drivers dread. Gridlock costs the customer dearly in extra time and costs the driver too if he's struggling to reach an impatient customer at a specified time.

Bear this in mind if you need a cab between 8 and 9, particularly on a Monday morning. Give yourself as much time as possible.

When the schools break up it's a different picture. There are almost no delays in the lighter traffic and cabs are sitting on ranks waiting for work. So, if you're looking for someone to blame, blame the parents.

Late Afternoon. School finishing time is also hectic but nothing like as bad as the morning. Blame this secondary chaos on

education authorities off-loading thousands of children at the same time. Coaches, buses, taxis are all pushed to the limit during a manic hour until the workload subsides to normal.

The demand during other times of the day doesn't create these shortfalls in service. A day-shift taxi driver working 5am to 5pm has only these two peak periods to cope with. The rest of the day sees cabs on every taxi rank in the city.

Evening. However in the 5pm-6pm Monday to Friday rush hour there can be delays for the taxi-travelling public. Mainly for two reasons. Firstly, traffic congestion again reduces the number of cabs available because so many drivers are bricked into traffic jams.
Secondly, as it's the end of the working day for day-shift drivers they'll all be making their way to garages to fuel up before handing their vehicles over to night-shift drivers, who won't be out in force until about 6.30.

Night Time. Not every night has a peak period but when it happens it's usually just as the pubs come out. Then you can see punters flagging down cabs in great desperation – as if they'd been waiting in vain in the cold for 45 minutes whereas in fact the same driver passed the same spot a minute before and saw no one.

Pubs and clubs now stagger their closing times so the workload for taxis is not what it was when everything closed at 11pm. Sunday to Thursday late-night clubbers are accommodated without much delay. It's when thousands of people are ejected onto the streets at the same time, all wanting cabs to take them home, that you've got problems. This is what happens in the early hours of Saturday and Sunday mornings when the big clubs close at 3am.

It's a busy time for every night-shift cabbie. The rail network will have closed down at 11pm. Glasgow's wonderful underground system, which has had millions injected into it, will have shut even earlier than the trains. The bus companies that supply a limited service at 3am can't cope with demand. The unlimited private hire cars on call at this time can't cope cither. Despite all the options that could be available, in the end it's down to to the taxi trade to clear the streets at this unsociable time of the night.

Though we're the only transport service in the whole of the city with enough drivers and vehicles on the streets at 3am to do the job, we're the ones to get most flack for doing too little.

Did you know that a member of the public who's had his car stolen will frequently offer us a reward of £50 or even £100 if we can spot the present whereabouts of the lost treasure? Instantly there'll be a team of a thousand drivers on the look-out and it's surprising how often a vehicle is located and the reward claimed.

VEHICLE AND DRIVER

A taxi is a unique form of public transport. It offers a personal service, taking you from door to door, unlike a train or a bus or an underground which takes from where you don't wish to be picked up to where you don't wish to go.

The cab itself stands out in the crowd, it's instantly recognisable, a purpose-built vehicle designed to meet the most rigorous of standards and provide a secure and private service.

Before being given a licence to drive a Glasgow cab, every applicant must sit a topographical or knowledge test. This assures customers of his thorough mastery of city streets and districts, the short cuts, the well-known commercial buildings, the places of interest, the hotels, the pubs and clubs, the hospitals, health centres and old folks' homes, the travel terminals, the undertakers, the cemeteries and crematoriums.

Once the test has been passed, it's the turn of Strathclyde Police to delve into the applicant's background and confirm or reject his application on the grounds of a criminal record. If the applicant does not meet the criteria of the police or licensing court then any such rejection will be upheld. The thought of this rigorous process is enough to put most undesirables off even attempting to join the trade – so the travelling public can have confidence when they step into a Glasgow taxi.

Taking customers from A to B is the bulk of our business, but it's by no means the only part of our daily routine. Students will often carry out a 'flitting', vacating one bedsit for another, and our vehicles will usually accommodate all their worldly goods, from clothing and bedding to computers, DVDs and strobe lighting. Accompanying every undergraduate flitting, large or small, is the heavy laundry basket filled to capacity in the absence of mother.

Health centres and hospitals also put business our way as we're able to accommodate patients with disabilities, with Zimmer frames or wheelchairs, when ambulances are under pressure. Doing the job of a small van, the cab is also frequently used to transport medical equipment, including breathing apparatus and oxygen cylinders, from hospital to hospital or to patients' homes. Medical specimens, X-rays, case notes, operating theatre equipment, doctors and nurses, the patients themselves – all are at times transported by taxi.

Using taxis for these purposes can be very cost-effective for hospitals as they only pay for the cabs as required, saving on staff downtime and vehicle running costs. Taxis can respond instantly to large hospitals as they're normally waiting on a rank within the grounds. Unless they're needed for a return journey, the cabs will of course only charge a one-way price – a saving in itself as a van coming back empty would still have to be paid for.

Then there are the courier services for businesses, delivering urgent packages and financial mail. Taking all these things together, we have quite a varied customer base.

But it is in the summer months, when there's hot weather and the pubs start to run dry of the refreshing liquid as they attempt to quench the thirst of every young buck out there, that our cabs get used for the most important missions of the year. We save many a Glaswegian life that might otherwise have been lost through dehydration by shuttling full kegs of beer and lager from pub to pub, preventing epidemics of thirst and saving the local breweries from humiliation.

To sum up, the taxi cab, a cross between a people carrier and a light van, with added refinements, is an on-the-spot vehicle, an instant-response unit for virtually any purpose imaginable.

Did you know that after the Second World War Austin became a major supplier of automobile engines to the Japanese conglomerate Nissan, exporting over two million power units?

Isn't it ironic that in 1988, British industry having failed to supply a reliable, environmentally-friendly engine for the new Fairway cab, we turned to Nissan?

It was during their co-operation in the 'fifties that Austin had educated Nissan designers and engineers in the art of manufacturing and designing the modern diesel engine. Between 1988 and 2001 all Fairway and TX1 taxi engines were fitted with the popular and well-proven Nissan diesel engine.

As a taxi driver's son brought up on the banks of the Clyde in Glasgow in the 1950s, I can clearly remember my mother telling us that the Japanese were over to visit Glasgow and were learning the shipbuilding trade from our own fine shipyards on the Clyde. She felt we were throwing away our knowledge to foreigners who would one day take over our industries and take our jobs to the other side of the world, leaving Glasgow's shipyards idle.

So convinced was she that this would happen that she quoted these words: 'Some day this disastrous exercise will come back and haunt us. Do you think that Japan would welcome us over there to learn their trade secrets? – I don't think so.'

So, fifty years later: no Linwood; no ships. Who's to blame?

All this from the wife of a Glasgow cab driver fifty years ago.

TRADE JARGON

Bare fare	Minimum price that must be paid
Bare hire	Hire without a tip
Begging light	Roof light indicating taxi for hire
Bucket seats	Two pull-down seats behind the driver
Bung	Gratuity
Call sign	Vehicle's identifying name
Change-over	Driver handing the cab over to his mate
Clear of fuel	Gross earnings less fuel
Clocked	Recorded by the taximeter
Controller	Person who despatches jobs
Drop the flag	Set the meter going
Dropped a hire	Completed a job
Dutted	Not paid for a hire
Feeder rank	Back-up rank serving main rank
Flag fall	Starting price on the meter
Flagging down	Hailing a cab
Fresh blood	New drivers
Game	Taxi business
In the saddle	Working the cab
Inspection	Thorough testing
Mobile	Driver
No job	Taxi phone hire not there
On the air	Working with two-way radio switched on
Over the air	Radio broadcasting
Paid off	Driver paid by customer at end of hire
Runner	Escaping non-payer
Signing on	Starting the shift
Sleepers	Passengers who fall asleep in the cab
Suicide doors	Doors that open into oncoming traffic
Weigh-in	Cab rental money
Working the street	Car without two-way radio